Hike
Lewis and Clark's
Idaho

Hike
Lewis and Clark's
Idaho

Mary Aegerter
Steve F. Russell

University of Idaho Press
Moscow, Idaho

First published 2002 by the University of Idaho Press

Printed in Canada

06 05 04 03 02   5 4 3 2 1

Library of Congress Cataloging-in-Publication Data
Aegerter, Mary.
  Hike Lewis and Clark's Idaho/ Mary Aegerter; Steve F. Russell.
    p. cm.
  Includes bibliographical references.
  ISBN 0-89301-257-2 (alk. paper)
    1. Lewis and Clark Expedition (1804–1806) 2. Hiking–Idaho–Guidebooks.
  3. Idaho–Guidebooks. I. Russell, Steve F. II. Title.

F592.7.A35 2002
917.804'2–dc21

                                2002002827

Interior photographs by Warren Case
Visit our website at www.uidaho.edu/uipress

To Sean and Liam, and to the unnamed and unknown people who have traveled the Lolo Trail in past centuries.

Contents

You are about to visit a special place, an area that looks almost the same as it did when Meriwether Lewis, William Clark, and the Corps of Discovery passed through in 1805 and 1806. Not in any one place, of course, but in the general mix of landscapes, and because it's largely undeveloped, as it surely was then. You'll see evidence of both, even if you stay on Highway 12, the main road through this section of Idaho.

Highway 12 is just two lanes wide, with narrow shoulders. It's bounded on one side by steep hills and by the Lochsa River for much of the way on the other side. Between Lolo, Montana, and Kooskia, Idaho, motorist services are minimal—a few restaurants and gas stations, and more campgrounds than motels.

What you'll find is an imposing landscape, a mix of treed, open, and brushy slopes, with rock outcroppings interspersed. The steep slopes coming down to the highway, the rivers, and the streams are called breaklands or simply "the breaks." They charge down in grades of 60 percent and more. The trees clinging to their sides are primarily Western red cedar in the wetter areas, grand fir or Douglas fir elsewhere. Most of the big game in the area live in the breaklands.

The Lolo Motorway travels the middle and upper slopes of the ridges on the north and northwest side of the highway. It's steep here too, and the hills are dissected by the beginnings of the many streams that rush down to join the Lochsa. On top, however, the slopes are gentler, more stable. Red cedar grow there, as do grand fir, mountain hemlock and, at the higher elevations, subalpine fir. There are subalpine meadows along the Motorway, and glimpses of rugged rocky areas above tree line to the east and south.

At the western edge of the Lolo corridor, you'll travel through rolling hills and relatively flat plateaus, areas with slopes of less than 30 percent.

But there's something besides the landscape that's special about this place. As a result of its rugged terrain, relative isolation, and lack of development, hiking here is not like hiking other places you may have visited.

First, you are unlikely to meet others along the trail, especially those off the Motorway. Although Mary hiked these trails prior to the bicentennial, she met other hikers on just nine of the trails in this book. On two of those, the people were outfitters, and three of the other seven trails are either extremely short or heavily used.

Second, the Motorway travels the remote ridges north of the Lochsa River, and it easily could take more than one day for help to arrive, should you need it and be able to send for it. There are no cell phone towers, and radio communication is difficult, if not impossible, even for the Forest Service.

Third, hiking off Highway 12 or the Motorway often involves significant exertion, elevation gains in excess of 3,000 feet for trails that climb either to the Motorway or, on the other side of the Lochsa River, to the near ridge of the Selway-Bitterroot Wilderness.

Fourth, the trails are often in less-than-perfect condition. The tread can be as narrow as six inches wide, and some trails are along steep hillsides with steep drop-offs. Vegetation can be enthusiastic and overhang the trail, interfering with your ability to see where to put your feet. Trees fall across the trails at all times of year, even after the Forest Service has cleared the winter and spring downed trees. There may be tree roots and rocks of all sizes within the trail path, and, especially on trails heavily used by horses or mechanized vehicles, the tread may be a rut many inches below the surrounding ground.

Finally, historical trails in some places are left in historical condition rather than brought up to current standards.

For these reasons, please approach your visit here with the Boy Scouts' motto firmly in mind, "Be Prepared." Then set out and enjoy the small part of Idaho that Lewis, Clark, and the Corps of Discovery traveled in 1805 and 1806.

—MARY AEGERTER

—STEVE F. RUSSELL

Whenever a book is written, it is usually the sum total of the input the author has received from many people over the course of many years. That is what makes an acknowledgment so important and yet so difficult. First of all, I thank my coauthor Mary. Her energy, dedication, and perseverance made it successful. I also thank the University of Idaho Press for appreciating the merits and value of a hiking book for the historic Clearwater country. People who have confidence in my trail research or may have been especially encouraging over the years are Jim Fazio, Tom Geouge, Larry Jones, Bud Moore, Gary Moulton, Deanna Reibe, Jim Ronda, Rebecca Russell, Ralph Space, Mike Venso, Merle Wells, and Sam Wormley. I gratefully acknowledge them. Finally, my family deserves my most sincere gratitude for their efforts in cheerfully putting up with my long summer absences.

—Steve F. Russell

The impetus for writing this book was a Forest Service employee who was lost for several days while trying to follow historic trails in the region. His experience was a call to action for many who live between Lolo Pass and Lewiston, Idaho. Dan Davis of the Clearwater National Forest put the bee in my bonnet for the book. It flew sluggishly at first, then with more enthusiasm as it became clear that a book covering trails that could be hiked safely would be a good idea. The collaboration between Steve and I came after a year of infrequent e-mails that were frequently misunderstood.

All of the hiking and all of the writing is mine. Steve provided the elevation profiles and the base maps. He also gave freely of what he's learned over his many years of historic trails research in the form of copious amounts of history and answers to my innumerable questions about the same—in short, everything that makes this book more than just a hiking guide. I thank him most of all.

Many other people helped with the preparation of this book. First and foremost were Sandy Bailey, Teresa Baker, Leanne Parker and Randy Robinson, each of whom gave several days of their vacation time to hike trails off the Lolo Motorway with me. Daughter Leslie McDonough and brother John Aegerter read the whole thing. Don Coombs chauffeured my first Motorway trip and provided years of editing help and outdoor mentoring. And a whole slew of people from the Clearwater National Forest gave freely of their time and expertise, especially Linda Fee and Tim Lewis, but also Jim Beale, Vern Bretz, Dan Davis, Sandi McFarland, Ken Rinehart, and Sarah Walker. Thanks to Candace Akins for a final round of organizational details during the book production process.

If in putting it all together, there are mistakes—they are mine alone, and I apologize for them.

—Mary Aegerter

Hike
Lewis and Clark's
Idaho

Much of the land traveled by the trails in this book is of spiritual
or sacred significance to the Nez Perce and other
Native American tribes.

Please travel it with this in mind.

Please do not disturb artifacts and other signs of use or
previous passing.

Federal law protects cultural sites and artifacts on public land via the
Archaeological Resource Protection Act, and violation of this act
carries severe penalties.

The Bitterroots have been crisscrossed with trails since they were first inhabited. Animals left the initial tracks, their trails tracing routes to water, to feed, and to shelter. Then came trails made by people who traveled the area on foot, sometimes using dogs to help carry their food and supplies. They left but faint traces of their passing in the dirt. The arrival of the horse in the early 1700s, and the increased amount of travel that resulted from their use, led to trails that were deeply eroded in the soft, granitic soils.

The early human trails were different than those we travel today. They followed the ridge lines rather than detouring around the high points as do our roads and trails. Often, the direct route over the ridge was the shortest and fastest, and the ridge lines were easier to follow. The trails also stayed up and out of the valleys unless there was no choice, for the hard, unyielding granite rocks gave rise to rugged ridges and narrow, steep canyons that were difficult, if not impossible, to travel.

These early trails were used by Native Americans and other travelers until the twentieth century, when the technology for building roads along the creek bottoms was developed. Once those roads were in use, most of the old trails were largely forgotten, except for the ancient Lolo Trail.

What we call the Lolo Trail is actually a trail system rather than an individual trail. The term is generic and has been used since the late 1800s to denote the route from Lolo, Montana, to Weippe, Idaho, via Lolo Pass.

■ The first Lolo Trail was that of the Northern Nez Perce, and it was used primarily by them and the Bitterroot Valley Salish. This is the trail that Lewis and Clark followed most of the time. The Bird-Truax Trail, built in 1866, followed the same route as the Northern Nez Perce Trail, but used a wagon grade. The erosion traces of the two trails coincide only where the ridge is narrow and flat.

■ The Bird-Truax Trail was the result of a Congressional appropriation for the purpose of building a wagon road to link the commercial interests of Lewiston, Idaho, with the gold mining interests of Virginia City, Montana. (The expedition that worked on it also was called the Lewiston and Virginia City Wagon Road Expedition.) Wellington Bird was the supervisor and disbursing agent hired to head the project. Major Sewell Truax, once commander of Fort Lapwai, was hired by Bird to supervise the wagon road building.

Surveying and construction began early in the summer of 1866. Bird soon realized that the road could not be built for the $50,000 appropriation, but that it would be possible to do the survey and perhaps build a trail. It took more than a month to complete the survey for a grade suitable for a wagon road. Steve's research indicates they then were able to clear that route to the width of a wagon road from Musselshell, possibly all the way to Sherman Peak. East of that, they cleared a minimum pack trail.

The Bird-Truax Trail was used for more than 60 years as the main route through the central Bitterroot Mountains. In the many places where its erosion trace is deep, it still can be seen.

■ The Lolo Trail National Historic Landmark also is a Lolo Trail, but the documents that created it were not specific as to which erosion trace it recognized.

■ The Lewis and Clark National Historic Trail is essentially the erosion trace of the Northern Nez Perce trail as it existed in 1805–1806.

■ The Nez Perce National Historic Trail, which commemorates the 1877 war and flight, is the trail that was used that year by the Nez Perce and the U.S. Army. It generally follows the 1866 Bird-Truax Trail. (See hike 40.)

Note: Ralph Space, former Clearwater National Forest supervisor and Lewis and Clark scholar, gives two different explanations for the name Lolo. The first suggests that it is the Flathead pronunciation for a trapper named Lawrence. The second, that it is a corruption of the French name Le Louis, the name French trappers gave to Lolo Creek and Lolo Pass to honor Meriwether Lewis.

The U. S. Forest Service began using the Bird-Truax/Lolo Trail route about 1907, in the early days of fire suppression. Fire suppression necessitated lookouts and the ability to reach and supply them, as well as a network of trails that allowed rapid access to fires while they still burned small. The Forest Service adopted the Lolo Trail route where it was convenient, and built new trails where it was not convenient or did not go. They reopened the Bird-Truax Trail as the main trail from Montana to Musselshell via Powell, Idaho. As more lookouts were built, more trails were added to the system until the 1950s, when new fire-fighting technology made the lookouts obsolete.

Fire not only helped preserve a portion of the ancient trail system, it also influenced its character. Fire cleared the underbrush, making travel easier, and we know that the Nez Perce used fire to keep the ridges clear.

However, fire could weaken trees so they were more easily blown down in storms, becoming the windfalls that made it impossible to get a horse safely through.

Today, almost a century of fire suppression has left us with trails that can be brush-choked. They must be cleared periodically or become impassable.

The use and maintenance of the trail system by the Forest Service helped preserve the Bird-Truax Trail and some small segments of the ancient route. What remains of it is used primarily for recreation, and it is maintained by hunters, other recreational users, and the Forest Service.

Between 1929 and 1934, the Forest Service and the Civilian Conservation Corps constructed a one-lane "truck trail" along the route of the Lolo Trail, generally parallel to but seldom actually on the Bird-Truax survey line, from Powell, Idaho, to Musselshell Meadows. It is what we now know as the Lolo Motorway. It was completed in the fall of 1934 and opened in the summer of 1935. Steve's grandfather outfitted out of Green Saddle and Howard Camp at that time, and he followed the road construction to its end each year.

Today, the Motorway and the trails leading off it are quiet for 10 months of the year. In the mid 1980s, when Steve began his trail research, he easily could spend a week along the Motorway without seeing another person or vehicle. By the late 1990s, it has become common to see one or two vehicles each day during the summer, most out huckleberry picking or following the route of Lewis and Clark. The exception, both then and now, is fall hunting season when the Motorway becomes a linear city, with hunters camped at all possible spots along its length.

Highway 12 is now the main "trail" through the area, and in a sense, it is the realization of President Jefferson's dream of a land bridge between the drainages of the Missouri and Columbia Rivers.

The road was started about 1925, as a one-lane dirt road from Lolo Hot Springs, over Lolo Pass, and down to the Crooked Fork of the Lochsa. It was extended to Powell between 1926 and 1928, after which construction on the east end stopped until the completion of a pioneer road from Powell to Papoose Creek. (A pioneer road is used during road construction for moving in equipment to cut and remove trees so that actual work on the roadbed can begin.)

Steve's grandfather and father cleared the first right-of-way from Powell Junction down the river. Construction was slow and expensive, and the working season was short. One winter the two were hired to keep the road plowed from the pioneer road east to Lolo Hot Springs so that work could begin as early as possible the following spring.

The road from the west was constructed primarily to provide access to timber harvest areas and to provide a supply road to what now is the historic Lochsa Ranger Station. By about 1920, a narrow dirt road reached Pete King Ranger Station, where the highway maintenance station now stands. Some parts of that section of the road were constructed by hand with pick and shovel. The road was continued on to Bimerick Creek in 1924, but no farther until 1941, when it was extended to Wildhorse Creek. It reached Fish Creek in 1951, Bald Mountain Creek in 1955.

The impetus to complete Highway 12 came in the early 1950s when the interstate highway system was built in response to national defense considerations. The final push came in the late 1950s, and the road was dedicated at Lolo Pass in 1962. Steve's grandfather was invited to and attended the dedication.

A Brief History of the Area

When Lewis and Clark crossed Lolo Pass on Friday, September 13, 1805, and entered what is now Idaho, they entered a place that had been lived in and traveled for thousands of years.

Some of those who preceded them may have been the descendants of the people who migrated over the land bridge that existed more than 13,000 years ago across the Bering Sea between Asia and Alaska. Certainly Native Americans such as the Shoshone and Bitterroot Salish have lived in and near the Bitterroots for thousands of years, and the Nez Perce have occupied this land since the beginning of their people. More abundant human habitation, however, has come during the last few hundred years, after the climate warmed and the winters shortened.

The early inhabitants fished the streams, harvested berries and roots from the ridges and sidehills, and hunted game when and where it was available. They camped throughout the area and spent time in places of spiritual significance. Their travel was slow and difficult at first, for all supplies and possessions were either hand carried or packed on dogs. They lived off the land after their supplies were used, which was a difficult undertaking, especially during late spring. The Nez Perce and Salish even peeled the bark off trees to reach the cambium layer and chewed it for its sugar content.

The arrival of the horse in the early 1700s led to dramatic changes, for it became possible to carry the food and supplies necessary for longer journeys. The Nez Perce then were able to travel hundreds of miles into central Montana to join the Salish and to hunt buffalo.

The first written information about the area came from the journals of members of the Corps of Discovery: Lewis, Clark, Patrick Gass, John Ordway, and Joseph Whitehouse.

Lewis and Clark's hopes were high when they entered Idaho; the road they traveled was very fine, level, open, and firm, according to Lewis. They camped at the lower end of Packer meadows, near Lolo Pass, and expected to cross the mountains they saw before them to the west in no more than four days. Things changed rapidly.

The next day it rained, snowed, and hailed on them, and their guide mistakenly led them down the salmon fishing trail to the Lochsa River instead of staying on the main route along the ridges above the river. They camped, tired and hungry, near the junction of the two creeks, now known as the Crooked Fork and Colt Killed Creek, that join to become the Lochsa. They killed and ate a colt that night, the first of three that sustained them through "these terrible mountains."

Their trip the next day from the Lochsa up to the ridgetop is known for the loss of Clark's desk. The climb was steep, and there was a great deal of fallen timber. Several horses fell that day, including the one with Clark's desk and small trunk. Luckily, the horses were not injured. The group camped that night at Snowbank Camp, where they used snow to make water and then soup from the remains of the colt. (Note: Most of the Lewis and Clark camps were named by the USFS more than 150 years after the Corps of Discovery's journey.)

Then it grew worse. There was snow that night and during the days to follow, more fallen timber, more steep trails, and no game. The route was sometimes difficult to find, narrow, rocky, or on the edge of a steep precipice. They camped at Lonesome Cove, near Indian Post Office, on September 16 and at Indian Grave Camp, near the Sinque Hole, on September 17.

Lewis and Clark split on September 18, the latter going ahead with six men to hunt. Clark camped on Hungery Creek that night, Lewis near Sherman Peak.

Clark was almost out of the mountains on September 19, camping near the Lewis and Clark Cedar Grove on Cedar Creek, while Lewis camped on Hungery Creek. Lewis camped on the ridge above Salmon Trout camp on September 20 and on Lolo Creek near Lolo Campground the next night. By September 22, both were out of the mountains. Each met the Nez Perce on the Weippe prairie and was given much-needed food: camas and salmon. Unfortunately, all members of the Corps had difficulty digesting these previously unknown-to-them foods.

Their return trip in 1806 went better, for they had three Nez Perce guides who knew the route well and knew where to find grass for the horses. But prior to that trip, they had made an impatient, too-early start east and were turned back by deep snow in the mountain ridges near Hungery Creek. During their successful trip they camped on Hungery Creek June 25, at Bald Mountain the next night, at Bears Oil and Roots Camp at Spring Mountain on June 27, 13-Mile Camp on June 28, and at Lolo Hot Springs in Montana on June 29.

There were many reasons the Corps' journey through these mountains was so difficult, and certainly the terrain was one of them. There was no single pass that would take them from one side of the Bitterroots to the other, that is, from the Missouri River drainage to that of the Columbia. When they crossed Lolo Pass, they could not continue along the two-lane highway that parallels the Lochsa, as travelers today can. There was not even a trail along the river in 1805–1806, just the Northern Nez Perce Trail, which was comprised of erosion traces along the ridgetops that had been followed by the ancient Native Americans. These ridgeline traces translated into a great deal of steep up and down travel across six major and many more minor saddles. There was snow, early and late, during the years they traveled, for the ridges are high enough through this corridor that snow can stay into July and return in September. Timber was dense, and usually much blew down during the winter. And there was little or no game on the ridge at that time.

It did not take long after Lewis and Clark returned east for increasing numbers of white men and women to move into the area. Many who came were explorers, trappers, and miners, but there were also surveyors, settlers, and military men. Several fur companies launched an intense competition—"fur wars"—and most early whites who came to the area were, in fact, trappers.

England and the United States competed to claim the vast lands of the Pacific Northwest. Not only were there huge profits to be made from fur trapping and trading with the local tribes but also each country desired the territory. Both wished to lay claim to the land, completely ignoring that it already was occupied by the tribes of the Northwest.

The miners who came were not terribly successful in the Lolo Trail area. Some old placer mining water ditches can be found meandering through the forest above Musselshell Meadows, evidence of mining along Musselshell Creek. Rhodes and Williams Peaks were named for Billy Rhodes and Lafe Williams, who worked the Blacklead Mountain area for silver. Nearby Cayuse Creek was named by two men who worked with Rhodes, for the colt or "cayuse" they found there.

Jerry Johnson worked the Bitterroot mountains, mining and trapping. He spent many years searching for Isaac's or the Lost Mine. Johnson learned of the supposedly rich gold mine from Isaac Hill, who told him that the gold there had been found by accident during the building of a sweat lodge some years earlier. Johnson hired Hill to guide him to the location, but Hill, after pointing to a peak covered with snow, died before reaching it. Johnson searched several summers for the mine, without luck. Many others have searched since then with the same result.

Loggers also came to the area, but sales of timber from the National Forest were small until the 1940s wartime economy brought high prices. Timber harvest brought road building. Blister rust devastated the white pine timber stands and resulted in the cutting of essentially all the commercial-grade white pine, while spruce bark beetles led to timber cuts in the 1950s. In August 1953, Steve's grandfather logged the first advertised commercial National Forest timber sale in the upper Lochsa, on the Idaho side of Lolo Pass. This was just the beginning of a massive timber cut that has far exceeded the sustainable yield in that country. As you hike the Lolo Trail area, you will see the extent of the upper Lochsa cuts, now primarily brush-choked hillsides.

Prior to 1953, Steve's grandfather had sawmills at Weippe and Musselshell, Idaho, and the small mill pond at Musselshell is still used by a large variety of wildlife. He harvested cedar poles at Crane Meadows, on state land about 10 miles southeast of Weippe.

The area remains sparsely populated, and many who live here have made a living from timber; some, from ranching or farming; others from the tourists that come, recognizing the special character of the land.

Geologic forces have taken billions of years to create the terrain that caused so much difficulty for Lewis and Clark on their journey through Idaho's Bitterroot Mountains.

The outermost layer of the Bitterroots is part of the 60-mile-thick continental crust. The crust is made up of several layers, and the topmost formed when a shallow sea covered the area for about 800 million years. During that time, sediment accumulated in the sea and became the sedimentary rock layers geologists call "belt rock." The older layers of rock beneath the belt rock are called "basement rock."

The continental crust or plate can be thought of as a raft of relatively light rocks floating on much heavier and denser rocks below. Continental plates and oceanic plates form a network that surrounds the world, and together they make up the rigid outer layer of the earth.

About 700 to 800 million years ago, a split, or rift, occurred in the continental plate near what is now the western border of Idaho. When a rift occurs, the plates move away from each other, and a broad gulf forms that eventually becomes a sea.

Western Idaho was part of the North American west coast for the 700 million years or so that followed the rift. Toward the end of that time, another rift developed, this time in what is now the Atlantic Ocean. As the mid-Atlantic rift widened, the continental plate was pushed west. At roughly the same time, the oceanic plate in what is now the Pacific Ocean was being pushed east. The two collided about 200 million years ago.

When continental and oceanic plates collide, the heavier oceanic plate is driven down and under the continental plate. The process is not smooth, and the rigid continental plates become compressed, buckled, and bent during the process.

Numerous plate collisions, large and small, filled Idaho with a great deal of granite, added islands to the coast, and created the Northern Rocky, Clearwater, and Bitterroot Mountains. The collision of about 200 million years ago started the formation of those mountain ranges.

The oceanic crust that was forced down and under the continental crust eventually melted into basalt magma. That magma in turn heated the continental crust above it, parts of which recrystallized into gneisses and schists. As the heat became more intense, the gneisses and schists closest to the magma melted and mixed, forming granite magma.

According to one popular geologic theory, the granite magma rose up into the welt under the mountains and caused the rocks above it to fracture and slide east in big slabs, becoming the Northern Rockies as we know them. Because the covering rocks slid east, the deep rocks were exposed. That rock, the granite magma, had cooled slowly underground and under pressure, and became the Idaho batholith, which is the rock we see now in much of the Bitterroot and Clearwater Mountains.

As the granite magma rose, it also dragged some of the gneisses and schists with it, and we see them at the borders of the Idaho batholith. An alternate theory suggests that the gneisses and schists may have once been sedimentary belt rocks.

About 100 million years ago, vagrant Pacific islands collided with the west coast. They were too light to sink under the continental crust, so they just latched on. You can see them—the Wallowa and Seven Devil Mountains—at the northeast Idaho–Oregon border, overlooking the Snake River.

During the Eocene period, 45–55 million years ago, granite and other fine-grained rocks intruded into the existing rock of the upper Lochsa and North Fork of the Clearwater near Lolo Pass. The molten rocks filled in fractures in the older, existing rock, forming narrow dikes or larger intrusions called stocks.

Weathering during the next 30 million years created a hill and valley topography that was later inundated by the Columbia basalt flows of 15 to $17\frac{1}{2}$ million years ago. The flows filled valleys, covered low ridges and knolls, and isolated higher areas along the western edge of the Clearwater Mountains. The warm, humid climate during this period led to rapid weathering of exposed rocks and the creation of soil.

Once the flows stopped, the ground above the exhausted magma pool sank, forming the Clearwater basin near Lewiston, Idaho, and Clarkston, Washington. Rocks along the western edge of the Clearwater Mountains tilted toward that sinking basin, creating increased stream gradients and promoting erosion.

When the climate cooled about 100,000 years ago, mountain cap and alpine cirque glaciation sculpted the higher elevations of the Clearwater and Bitterroot Mountains. The mountain cap glaciers helped round the tops of some of the mountains, and the alpine glaciers carved away at other mountains, steepening their side slopes and forming the small basins that now hold high mountain lakes. The few steep, rocky mountain tops in the area are the Selway Crags, Bitterroot Mountain peaks, and some of the high area above Silver and Kelly Creek drainages. The glaciers receded as the climate warmed, disappearing around 10,000 years ago.

The eruption of Mt. Mazama about 6,600 years ago deposited ash over a large area that included the Clearwater and Lochsa drainages. Since then, landslides and erosion by water have been the primary means of geologic change.

The area traversed by the Lolo Trail has four warm-water spring formations: Lolo Hot Springs, Jerry Johnson Hot Springs, Colgate Licks, and Weir Creek Hot Springs.

Geological features to look for while driving or hiking

The border zones between batholith and metamorphic rocks can be seen along Highway 12 near Lolo Pass, milepost 174, and near Glade Creek, mileposts 103–104. Most of the metamorphic rocks are gneiss or schist. In general, metamorphic rocks look layered, streaky, or swirly. Some have veins of granite. Feldspar, pinkish crystals set in dark mica, and pegmatite veins, visible as pinkish streaks, can be seen.

There are pegmatite dikes and crystals of light green beryl in the rock slide at milepost 164 on Highway 12.

Just west of Old Man Creek, near milepost 113 on Highway 12, there are bright green roadcuts with green diopside, a metamorphic limestone.

The Idaho batholith is visible for about 40 miles along Highway 12, from Old Man Creek to Powell. It is a pale gray rock that weathers to pinkish brown.

The dikes and stocks of the Eocene intrusion can be seen along Highway 12 near Lolo Pass. The Eocene rocks look pink rather than gray when freshly broken, and the grains are larger. Basalt dikes can be seen on Highway 12 from below Sherman Peak to below Grave Butte, roughly between mileposts 120–135.

The old Idaho coastline rocks can be seen in the mylonite rocks that surround the visitor center at Dworshak Dam above Orofino, Idaho. Mylonite is metamorphic rock that was sheared when it was still hot enough to flow. It is linear looking and slabby, like flagstones.

Terms and Definitions

Andesite A volcanic rock, intermediate in composition between basalt and rhyolite, found in shades of gray or brown along the eastern part of the Motorway.

Basalt A dark-colored, fine-grained igneous rock. It is the most common volcanic rock and is often seen in columnar form, each column having four to seven sides, most often five.

Batholith A large body of igneous rock with a surface area exceeding 40 square miles. The Idaho batholith is composed primarily of granite.

Feldspar A family of minerals that includes aluminum, silica, and sodium. It is the most abundant mineral family in the earth's crust. Orthoclase feldspar contains potassium and crystallizes into pink, beige, or white blocky grains. Plagioclase feldspar contains sodium and calcium and commonly crystallizes into white blocky grains. It is the most abundant feldspar.

Gneiss Metamorphic rock that contains a lot of feldspar and appears streaky. It looks similar to granite in the Bitterroots, except for the banding and the coarser graining.

Granite Igneous rock made of feldspars with quartz and mica or hornblende in crystals large enough to see with the unaided eye.

Hornblende A glossy black silicate mineral that crystallizes into long prisms.

Igneous Rock formed by the action of great heat within the earth.

Mica A group of silicate minerals with a flaky, layered structure.

Pegmatite An igneous rock with extremely large crystals and having the same mineral makeup as granite.

Quartz A clear, glassy mineral form of silicon dioxide.

Rhyolite A fine-grained, pale volcanic rock with the same composition as granite. It is the light gray to pinkish-gray rock found in great quantity along the Motorway.

Schist Metamorphic rock that contains either enough mica to appear flaky or enough needle-shaped minerals to appear splintery.

A list of especially recommended hikes is found between this section and the hikes section of the book. Check them out, especially if hiking time is limited. There may be little point in hiking up 3,000 feet of steep hillside if the views are limited, or it may be useful to know which historical trails are the most accessible, or have the best flowers.

Some trails are blazed. Blazes are marks on trees, usually made by removing bark but sometimes made with paint. They generally are found on both sides of a tree, near eye level, and look like an upside-down boot track— a small mark on top with a larger mark under it. These are called "candlestick blazes." Blazes that look like a right-side-up boot track are called "boot-track blazes," although I've rarely, if ever, seen the latter.

Each hike is organized in the same fashion.

■ **Why** do the hike? For views, for history, for wildflowers, or other points of interest.

■ **Ease:**

Easy hikes are short, usually less than 1 mile each way, and relatively flat, with an elevation change of less than 500 feet. They are also well-marked or very easy to follow.

Moderate hikes are 1 to 5 miles each way, with an elevation change of less than 1,500 feet.

Difficult or strenuous hikes are more than 5 miles each way, have an elevation change of more than 1,500 feet, or both.

The distance given is one-way unless otherwise noted.

■ **Season:** This indicates when the trail is free of snow and the trailhead is accessible in a normal year.

For all of the hikes with trailheads on Highway 12, the trails are open from early June through October. This is an average figure for the entire length of the road from Lolo to Kamiah. In reality, there is a great deal of yearly variation in when any one trail is open and in how far it might be free of snow. Trails near Kamiah will open earlier in the spring, probably by May during most years, while those near Powell may not open until late June. Trails on north-facing slopes will be open later in the spring than those on south-facing slopes. And, hiking uphill in the spring will always move you toward trail with more snow. Conversely, in the fall, trails near Kamiah close later, while those near Powell close earlier. Trails on north-facing slopes close earlier. And, hiking uphill brings you to snow earlier in the season.

Don't be put off, however, if you're traveling the area in April or even earlier. There are trails to hike this early, and the worst that can happen is that at some point along them, there will be too much snow to hike through. The best could be wonderful: early season wildflowers or wildlife not yet accustomed to having people around.

The high areas are usually accessible from July through September, while the Warm Springs Trail (hike 5) is used year-round, regardless of snow.

Campgrounds along the highway generally open for the Memorial Day weekend and close after Labor Day.

The same season has been listed for all of the hikes that originate on the Lolo Motorway—the time when you normally can drive the entire road. (The Lolo Motorway is Forest Road 500.) Hikes near the ends of the Motorway probably can be reached before then, however, though they certainly still will contain debris and fallen logs. Moon Saddle, about $28\frac{1}{2}$ miles along the Motorway, is the last place to be free of snow most years.

■ **Maps:** All of the hikes in Idaho along the Motorway and Highway 12 are within the Clearwater National Forest (CWNF). The hikes off the Selway River are within the Nez Perce National Forest (NPNF), and the hikes in Montana are within the Lolo National Forest (LNF). See the resource section for information on where to buy these forest maps.

United States Geological Service (USGS) maps that cover the area of each hike are noted. However, at this time and within the area covered by this book, USGS maps are available only at the CWNF office in Orofino, Idaho, and only maps covering the CWNF are sold there. See the resource section for information on where to order them.

■ **Information:** The Forest Service district or station that contains the hike and its phone number (as of 2001) is given. The address is found in the resource section.

■ **Trailhead:** Highway 12 has green mile markers at the edge of the road along its length. For hikes off that highway, the trailhead location is noted as being between two mile markers. If only one is given, the trailhead is essentially at that mile marker.

For hikes off the Motorway, the trailhead location is given as miles from the junction of Highway 12 and the Parachute Hill Road #569, which is the easternmost place of entry to the Motorway. Left and right directions are given for east to west travel.

Note: All of the historical trails along the Motorway have been marked by the Forest Service with a simple upright round post with a diagonally cut top. On the front there is a small, white, triangular sign or signs noting that the trail is Nez Perce (FS#40), Lewis and Clark (FS#25), or both. (There are no similar signs marking historical trails on Highway 12.) These trails travel the routes of the two historic trails rather than the actual tread, and they may or may not agree with the routes identified by others who have done historic trail research.

Historical trails are not open to any mechanized transportation, including bicycles.

■ **The Hike:** These descriptions are not step-by-step guides to the trails. My aim has been to provide enough information so that trails, or portions of trails, can be hiked without undue worry about getting lost or having problems, about game trails, or about meadows where the trail is less than distinct. But I trust that you'd realize fairly quickly if you've moved off the hiking trail and on to a game trail, if for no other reason than game often head straight up or down hills. Hikers usually don't.

Obvious landmarks are noted, as are mile markers or signs on trees. Additional information is included as to what the hike is like: is it in the woods or out in the open, are there long uphills or downhills, are there places that have views. Finally, distance information is given. It is limited, however, because I don't carry anything that directly measures distances. The numbers given are based on my average hiking speed.

In general, all trails are easy to follow the first mile or two because those sections are traveled with more frequency. And, in general, trails described as "secondary" or "way" are, at best, infrequently maintained.

Because I've hiked every mile of every trail in this book except for the last 3/4 mile of the No-see-um Butte Trail, there should be a high level of uniformity among hike descriptions, even given that I hiked with different people at different times and may have adjusted my speed accordingly, or that extreme weather and steep slopes have been known to affect my hiking speed.

Connections. When a trail goes farther than I've hiked or connects with other trails, that information is given. The connecting trail should not be used, however, without checking first with the Forest Service.

A case in point: When I hiked the Warm Springs Trail (hike 5), I met a young woman on her way out from her first backpack. She'd spent several days hiking alone in the Selway Bitterroot Wilderness. At the higher elevations she found that the trails on her forest maps weren't always there. She spent one entire day looking for a trail but not finding it and not knowing with certainty where she was. Luckily, she ended the day back where she started. She also crossed several creeks that were mid-thigh deep. She got herself into situations she wouldn't have if she had checked first with the Forest Service. (She also shouldn't have been out there alone, but that's another issue entirely, and she also should have carried USGS maps and a compass.)

When calling the Forest Service to check on trails and roads, keep in mind that the people answering the phone are doing their best to pass along information from trail maintenance workers, but probably haven't been out there themselves.

And because the hiking for this book was done in 2000 and 2001, expect that some things will have changed since then.

Maps. The trails are shown on scanned USGS maps, 7.5-minute series, reduced no more than 36 percent. They are sufficient for hiking the trails but contain only the area immediate to the trails. Maps that cover two pages will have a slight bit of overlap. Trails are labeled with the Forest Service trail numbers.

Elevation Profiles. The profiles are designed to help you "see" the trail as it hikes, the ups and downs along the way, in addition to providing a quick check of the hike's distance and total elevation change. They are consistent from hike to hike in that if lines of the same slope are shown on two profiles, the two bits of trail represented by those lines will have approximately the same grade.

Especially Recommended Hikes

If you have limited time or energy, or just want some pointers, here are Mary's recommendations.

For Scenery
   Highway 12: Hikes 11, 14, 18
   Motorway: Hikes 22, 24, 30, 34, 35, 36, 37

Best Trees or Woods
   Highway 12: Hikes 2, 17, 39a
   Motorway: Hikes 33, 38, 40j

Wildflowers
   Highway 12: Hikes 13 (June), 16 (April)
   Motorway: Hikes 8, 33

Family, Easy, or Short
   Highway 12: Hikes 1, 6, 12, 13 (partway), 19 (partway)
   Motorway: Hikes 21, 24, 28, 29, 30 (partway), 35, 36, 37

History
   Highway 12: Hikes 1, 2, 3, 6, 39, 42, 43, 44
   Motorway: Hikes 3, 21, 25 (especially), 29, 38, 39, 40

Wheelchair
   Highway 12: The river side of Hike 1 is wheelchair accessible.

Water Falls
   Highway 12: Hikes 5, 7, 10, 15

Just Plain Fine Hikes
   Highway 12: Hikes 2, 6, 8, 10, 13, 16, 19, 20
   Motorway: Hikes 8, 22, 25, 26, 38

The Hikes

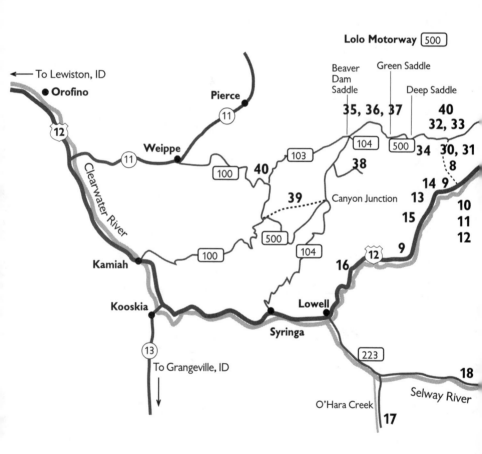

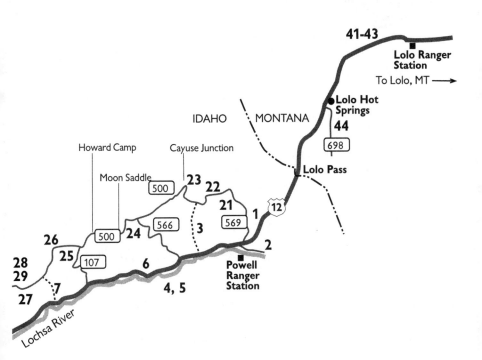

41-43

Lolo Ranger
Station

To Lolo, MT ⟶

IDAHO   MONTANA

Lolo Hot
Springs
44

698

Howard Camp   Cayuse Junction

Moon Saddle   23
500   22

21
566   3   569   1   12

26   24
500   2

28   25   107   6   Powell
29   Ranger
7   4, 5   Station
27

Lochsa River

Selway
Falls   20

Meadow   19
Creek

The DeVoto Cedar Grove FS#789

Why: Two short loops that wander through groves of large, old Western red cedar, which are up to 5 feet in diameter. The riverside loop is wheelchair accessible.

Ease: Easy. The accessible trail is level, the other loop has only a small bit of uphill. Both are short, under $1/3$ mile.

Season: Early June through October.

Maps: CWNF Visitor Map; USGS Rocky Point, Idaho. (The trails are not shown on either map, and maps are not necessary for this hike.)

Information: Powell Ranger District, CWNF, 208-942-3113.

Trailhead: The trailhead is at milepost 165 on Highway 12.

The Hike: The DeVoto Cedar Grove is named for author and Lewis and Clark scholar Bernard DeVoto, who was probably the first of the Lewis and Clark scholars to suggest that the viewpoints of the Native American tribes encountered by the expedition should be more fully explored. Ralph Space says that the grove was a favorite spot of DeVoto's during the time he was writing his edition of the journals of Lewis and Clark. DeVoto often camped here, when the area still included a campground, and sat under a massive cedar where he watched and listened to the Crooked Fork as he worked.

DeVoto died in 1955, and at his request, his ashes were scattered over the national forest. The cedar grove was named after him in 1960 when this section of Highway 12 was completed. The campground he used was removed during highway construction, as were some of the cedars. One of the cedars was dated at over five hundred years old.

The cedars along the trail on the river side of the road once held telephone insulators for the number nine telephone wire that ran from the upper Lochsa country to the public telephone network in Missoula, Montana. That wire was a vital link for the Powell Ranger District, Lochsa Lodge, and the numerous fire lookouts of that era.

Many visitors believe that Lewis and Clark passed through this grove or camped here. Neither is true. The trails they followed were atop the ridge to the north and south of the grove, and their nearest campsite was at what is now the Powell Ranger Station, near the junction of Colt Killed and Crooked Fork Creeks.

Steve's family passed through the DeVoto Grove in the 1950s, traveling to and from their home at Lochsa Lodge on the old, single lane dirt road that predated Highway 12. The giant cedars were shady and cool along what otherwise could be a hot and dusty road. Though the road is no longer dusty, the grove is still a fine place to visit, especially on foot.

The hard-surfaced trail on the river side of the highway features six spots with informative signs about the trees and the area. There is also a picnic spot with a table and a ramp down to the bank of the Crooked Fork. (The Crooked Fork joins with Colt Killed Creek about two miles downstream to become the Lochsa River.)

The trail on the opposite side is the longer of the two, and it is not paved. A sign at its start helps with the identification of a few flowers and ferns. The understory is low and bright green, a pleasant contrast to the gray-red trunks of the trees. This loop would be heaven if it was farther back so that road noise couldn't be heard.

Why: A level trail that provides easy access to a pleasant cedar woods, plus a chance to walk along the creek named by William Clark on September 14, 1805.

Ease: Easy to moderate, depending on how far you walk, with an approximate 600-foot elevation gain over the first 5 miles of trail.

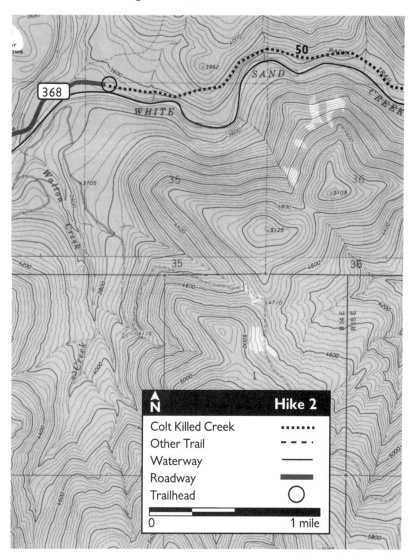

↑N	Hike 2
Colt Killed Creek	....
Other Trail	- - - ·
Waterway	——
Roadway	▬▬
Trailhead	○

0   1 mile

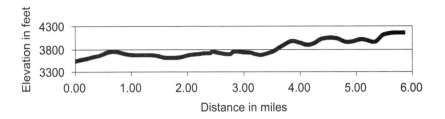

Season: Early June through October at the lower end; late June through September from Colt Killed Cabin.

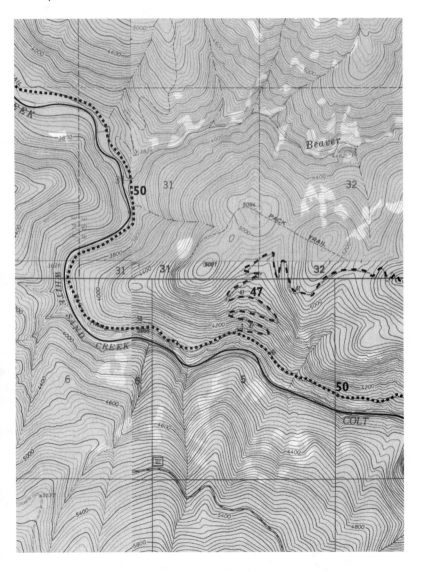

Maps: CWNF Visitor Map; USGS maps Grave Peak, Rocky Point, Roundtop, and Savage Ridge, Idaho.

Information: Powell Ranger District, CWNF, 208-942-3113.

Trailhead: Turn on to the Elk Summit Road at milepost 163–164 on Highway 12. Turn left after 1.1 miles on road #368. The trailhead is signed for White Sand on the right in another 0.6 mile. (This sign may be changed to Colt Killed by the time you hike here.)

The Hike: September 14, 1805, was a bad day for Lewis, Clark, and the other men of the Corps of Discovery. It rained, snowed, and hailed on them, depending on whether they were on the ridge or in the valley. They camped near today's Powell Ranger Station "much fatigued" and famished. Their hunters had been unsuccessful and "we wer compelled to kill a Colt . . . to eat . . . and named the south fork Colt killed Creek."

Regardless of Clark's having named it otherwise, the creek was known as White Sand Creek for over one hundred years, for the white, sandy beach on White Sand Lake, located in the creek's upper drainage. (A creek or river's drainage is the land area that drains water into that creek or river.) The name was changed to that given it by Clark in the late 1990s.

In the first mile of trail, there is a cedar woods with trees that reach 3 feet and greater in diameter. They are often in the company of a wide variety of other conifers, as well as abundant horsetail, and in one section, the only yellow and white columbine I've seen in the area.

Though the elevation gain over the first 5 to 6 miles of the trail is just a few hundred feet, the trail behaves as do most river trails in that it goes up and down many times. On this trail, most such deviations from the level are short, with the exception of one rather steep grade about 3 miles in.

For the first 2 miles, the trail returns to creek level after an uphill, sometimes to within touching distance of the water. Many of the wet areas are protected with wooden thoroughfares, which are elevated trail segments usually edged by logs. There are a couple of creeks to cross, Cabin and Beaver, and depending on the time of year, they might be deep enough to cause wet socks and feet.

After the steep uphill about 3 miles in, the trail crosses talus slopes and passes above and below rock walls. On occasion, there are views of the creek from this higher vantage point, including a couple of interesting-looking fishing holes. The trail intersects with the trail to Beaver Ridge in 4½ miles, by which time the trail definitely is showing signs of less use, but it is still blazed.

There are few views of anything but the creek and its close environs from this relatively narrow canyon—maybe a clear-cut on top of a nearby hill, or a road across a harvested area, or some undisturbed hillsides, still dark green with trees.

Connections: This trail is maintained as far as Colt Killed Cabin, 13 miles up the creek. The cabin at the top of the trail also can be reached by vehicle once Savage Pass and the 359 Road are open, which in normal years is in June.

The trail to Beaver Ridge, FS#47, is a secondary trail along the ridge and up to Road 369.

Why: Lewis and Clark traveled this trail on September 15, 1805, as their route from the Lochsa River Canyon up to the main ridge of the Lolo Trail. It was along this trail that several horses fell, including one that was carrying Clark's field desk.

Ease: Strenuous, with a 3,500-foot elevation change over the 7 miles of trail from Highway 12 to the Motorway. The trail need not be walked in its entirety, however. The first mile or two from either trailhead is evidence enough of why Lewis and Clark had difficulty ascending this ridge.

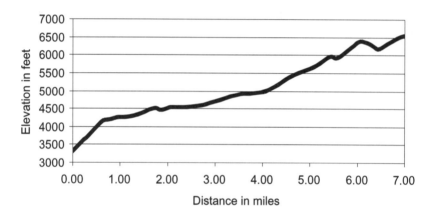

Season: Early June through October from Highway 12; mid-July through late September from the Motorway.

Maps: CWNF Visitor Map; USGS Cayuse Junction, Idaho.

Information: Powell Ranger District, CWNF, 208-942-3113.

Trailheads: The Highway 12 trailhead is on the right at mileposts 158–159. The Motorway trailhead is on the left at mile 12.8 on the Motorway. The best parking for the latter is a bit farther along the road at the sign for Snowbank Camp.

The Hike: The Lewis and Clark expedition climbed this trail starting at Whitehouse Pond on the Lochsa River and camping that night on the ridgetop at Snowbank Camp. At that time, the trail was probably a little-used Nez Perce diversion trail from the Lolo Trail to the fishing weirs at what is now Wendover Campground.

Both Lewis' and Clark's journals describe the country and trail in a negative manner, which is understandable without hiking the entire 7 miles. Clark said the trail wound in every direction in its attempt to get up the steep ascents, and that they passed an immense quantity of fallen timber.

Clark reported that on this day, the horse carrying his desk and small trunk fell off the trail, rolling 40 yards down the mountain until lodging against a tree. The horse escaped injury, but the desk did not.

That the trail was little used is evidenced by the difficulty Olin Wheeler and his guide had in trying to locate it during the late 1890s. Wheeler was documenting the trail for his books commemorating the centennial anniversary of Lewis and Clark's expedition, and the two found the trail faint or nonexistent.

When the Forest Service established a lookout near the trail's midpoint, the trail was reconstructed so that the lookout might be supplied either from the Lolo Trail or from Powell Ranger District via the Downriver Trail (hike 9). The trail has been used infrequently since the lookout was decommissioned and is of interest primarily to hunters and an occasional Lewis and Clark Trail hiker. The primitive character of the trail has definitely changed, however, because extensive logging has occurred in the areas close around it.

Wendover Ridge and Creek were named for Bert Wendover, a trapper who had a cabin near the creek's mouth.

There is a historical trail sign at the Highway 12 trailhead. The trail passes it, then crosses a short, flat area to reach a mileage sign indicating that Snowbank Camp is 7 miles away and Cayuse Junction, 10 miles.

The initial 3 or 4 miles of trail divides neatly into the two parts typical of many uphill hikes: getting to and then continuing uphill along the ridgeline. On this trail, the first of these is characterized by a series of switchbacks that tack up the steep slope. This section of trail is a bit narrow and slants to the outside, but there are occasional stretches with enough duff to make them as comfortable to hike as a trail can be. There's little scenery, just a variety of conifers with a low understory of grass and ferns. There are trail signs on both sides of the road that mark the trail's arrival at the ridgeline.

The lower section of the ridgeline trail also is typical, sometimes following the ridgeline, sometimes on its right, sometimes on its left. In a couple of places it runs through narrow tunnels of trees. In a few open spots, there are decent views up and down river, of Bear Mountain with its lookout downriver, and a nice stretch of the Bitterroot Divide upriver. Fortunately, there is little evidence of what's seen from higher up, close to the Motorway: the heavy human use that's occurred in the drainages on both sides of the ridge.

Hiking from the Motorway, and especially on the return trip uphill, there's a hidden benefit along this steep trail. The slope is not unrelenting, for the steep sections are separated into small, doable bits by short, relatively level segments. It's still a workout going up, but there will be some relief.

The trail travels from a mountain hemlock and Engelmann spruce forest

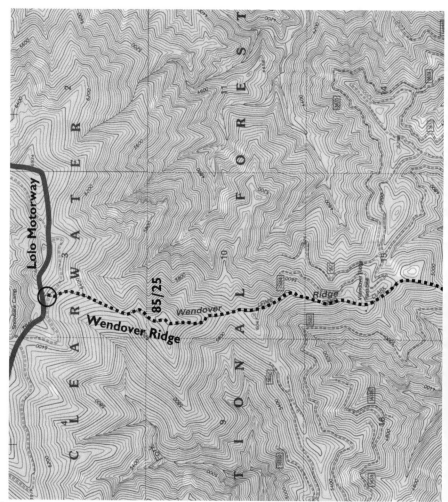

with a low understory of beargrass and whortleberry near the Motorway, down into a somewhat more standard Lochsa forest of Douglas fir, grand fir, larch, and ponderosa pine with a shrub understory. Among the wide selection of wildflowers, I saw baneberry (*Actaea arguta*) in late August, in both its color forms: some plants have red berries while others have white. In both cases, the loosely organized, oblong berry bunches sit high above the large, toothed, and divided leaves. (Note: All parts of the baneberry plant are considered highly poisonous.)

There are only one or two worthwhile views from this section of the hike, primarily of the Bitterroot divide. Here, however, the myriad of road cuts and other evidence of industrial logging are plainly visible in the foreground.

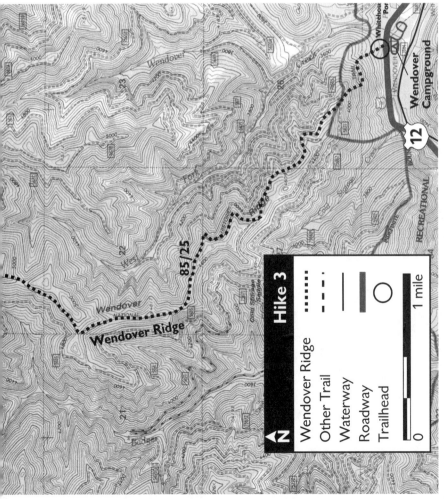

The top portion of the trail will have two versions by 2003: the actual trail, which is open to hikers, and a rerouted and more gently graded trail for stock. (There's no need to repeat the accident that befell Lewis and Clark.) The former is in decent shape throughout, not rutted but rocky in spots. The latter was not yet constructed in 2001.

Throughout the entire trail, there are several places with signs of old trail, diversions off the trail, or of a new trail to be constructed. Usually the old trails are obviously no longer used, and the diversions are short and return to the main trail within a few yards. Sometimes it's necessary to look around a bit to be sure you're really where you should be, that is, on the main trail.

Warm Springs Stock Bypass

via FS#44 and FS#46

Why: A cooler, less busy route to trail FS#49.

Ease: Easy, about 1¾ miles to the trail junction with FS#49 (hike 5), with little up or downhill.

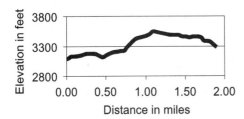

Season: Early June through October.

Maps: CWNF Visitor Map; USGS Bear Mountain, Idaho, and Tom Beal Peak, Idaho.

Information: Powell Ranger District, CWNF, 208-942-3113.

Trailhead: Mileposts 151–152 on Highway 12, at the Warm Springs Packbridge. The trailhead sign is across the bridge and locates this trail with a left-pointing arrow.

The Hike: The trail starts as a left turn at the trailhead sign across the Warm Springs Packbridge, heading upriver parallel to the highway and the Lochsa River for ¼ mile. Then it turns to the right at a sign to Warm Springs Trail #49, Stock traffic, and climbs a small hill. A second sign soon follows: Robin Ridge Trail #44, Warm Springs Stock Bypass. Hot Springs Lookout, left arrow. Warm Springs Packbridge, right arrow.

At the start of a second hill, a faint trail off to the right heads to what looks like a camping area. Stay to the left. From there on, the hike feels much like a walk in a pleasant, quiet park. The trees are primarily cedar, sometimes over 3 feet in diameter, with other species interspersed for variety. The understory is low, even sparse at times. The quiet is interrupted only by the sounds of Warm Springs Creek below as the trail heads down-

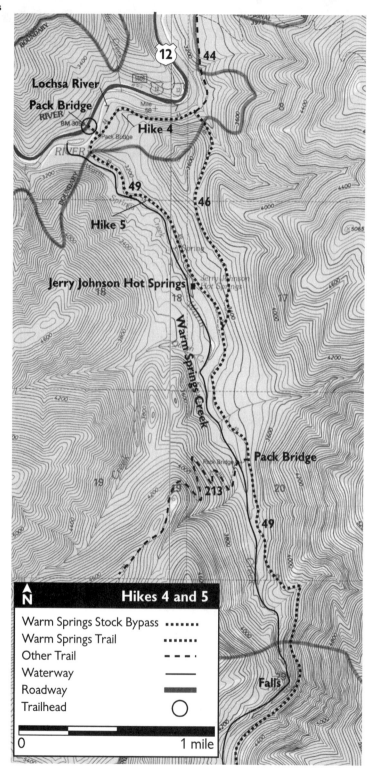

Lochsa River

Pack Bridge

Hike 4

Hike 5

Jerry Johnson Hot Springs

Warm Springs Creek

Pack Bridge

Falls

Hikes 4 and 5

Warm Springs Stock Bypass	••••••
Warm Springs Trail	••••••
Other Trail	‒ ‒ ‒ •
Waterway	——
Roadway	——
Trailhead	◯

N

0   1 mile

hill after crossing two wood bridges and just before connecting to trail FS#49 (hike 5).

While I don't usually hike trails where meeting stock is more likely than meeting hikers, I find that this trail provides a good alternative to the thoroughfare along Warm Springs Creek. The woods are pleasant, there are fewer people on it, and it avoids the always-busy hot springs. It would make a good circle hike of about $2^1/_2$ miles if combined with a right turn at the junction with FS#49 and a walk back through the hot springs to the trailhead.

Connections: The trail numbers may be confusing. The CWNF Visitor Map shows #44 as the trail that continues along the river to Hot Springs Point and does not show the #46 trail. The USGS map shows both trails but numbers the trail named Robin Ridge as #46. The trail to Hot Springs Point is a secondary trail.

Why: Jerry Johnson Hot Springs are just a 1-mile walk along a fairly level trail, and a waterfall is less than 4 miles in from the trailhead.

Ease: Easy to the hot springs; moderate with a 1,000-foot elevation gain over the 3½-plus miles to a view of the falls.

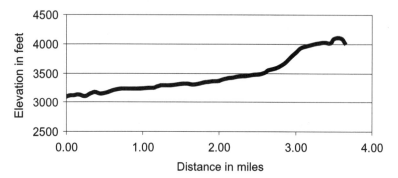

Season: The trail to the hot springs is used year-round, while that to the falls should be open from early June through October.

Maps: CWNF Visitor Map; USGS Bear Mountain, Idaho, and Tom Beal Peak, Idaho.

Information: Powell Ranger District, CWNF, 208-924-3113.

Trailhead: At the Warm Springs Packbridge, mileposts 151–152 on Highway 12. The trailhead sign is across the river, and this trail is a right turn at that point. (See page 34 for map.)

The Hike: The trail from the river to the hot springs has existed for at least several hundred years. Lieutenant C. P. Elliott traveled the trail and mapped the surrounding country during August and September of 1894 while he was searching for the body of George Colgate, the man left behind by the Carlin hunting party the previous autumn. (See hike 6.) During the late 1800s, the federal government also explored the Lochsa and Selway River drainages to prepare for the creation of the Bitterroot Forest Preserve that predated the Selway-Bitterroot Wilderness.

The springs are named for Jerry Johnson, the first white man to live in the area. Johnson was a prospector and trapper who lived on the north side of the Lochsa River, at the site of today's Jerry Johnson campground. Johnson was born in Prussia and emigrated to New Zealand in his youth, where he became interested in mining. He spent the rest of his life prospecting in wild, unpopulated places, sometimes also working as a guide, packer, or hunter.

It is said that Jerry Johnson told the Carlin party of a lost Nez Perce gold mine in the Warm Springs Creek area, a tale that has persisted to modern times and that is bolstered by occasional claims of gold traces. If there actually was a gold mine there, it is unlikely that Johnson would have told strangers. In those days, miners sometimes mysteriously disappeared after they revealed their gold diggings. The same was true for those who tried to follow a miner to his diggings.

> Colgate Licks and Warm Springs Creek were popular elk hunting areas when Steve's family purchased the Lochsa Lodge from Andrew Erickson in the 1940s. Both areas were part of the large outfitting area that came with the lodge. When Steve was 12 years old, his family took horses down the river on a hunting trip and stayed in an old cabin near where Jerry Johnson had lived. They hunted at Colgate and up the trail past the Jerry Johnson Hot Springs. Steve still remembers the fog generated by the hot water in the springs on that very cold fall day.
>
> In those days, the road along the river had not been built, and there was no public activity at the springs. After Highway 12 was constructed, the trail to the springs was improved and the alternate trail constructed to separate horse and foot traffic up Warm Springs Creek. Since then, books written on hot springs have guided many visitors to the area. Some damage has occurred because of the building of hot pools, and nude hot-tubbing is a common occurrence at the springs.

The word "Lochsa" means rough water. Lieutenant Elliot's map carries an interesting spelling of the river, *Loxaw*, and the oldest map of the area spells it *Lasus*.

In the early years, Jerry Johnson Hot Springs and Colgate Licks were referred to as the upper and lower warm springs, respectively. The creek retained the name Warm Springs Creek.

If you like walking through cedar woods on a wide, easy trail where you'll meet people and find hot springs to soak in, the first mile of this hike is for you. This trail is so well used from the trailhead sign across the pack bridge to the springs, it's difficult so see how anyone could lose it, even if they closed their eyes.

There are hot springs that essentially sit in Warm Springs Creek, and others that sit in a basin a bit farther along. I've always found them to be odd spots, probably in part because I lived in the staid, old Boston area for twenty-five years. The springs are used by the young and the old, the dressed and the undressed and the partially dressed. I prefer to hike the much quieter stock trail (hike 4) that starts at the trailhead sign and rejoins this trail just past the hot springs. It's my preference because I don't soak in hot springs and because if I hike the Warm Springs Trail, I see more people in a few minutes than I see in a whole year's worth of hiking anywhere else.

The trail becomes less distinct than it might be as you pass through the springs basin, for people walk every which way through that area. Once past the basin, however, it is again wide and easy to follow. For the rest of the hike, it spends most of its time in the trees, in shade with filtered sunlight and a low understory, in the quiet except for the noise of the creek.

The stock trail comes in from the left not far past the basin, and an apparent fork in the trail follows soon after. The right fork heads down to the creek, so take the left. Less than a half mile farther, the trail crosses Cooperation Creek. In late June it can be a bit deep to wade without getting wet socks. Luckily, there is a series of well-placed, hatched logs that make a dry crossing.

In another $1/4$ mile the trail splits. The right fork heads off to cross Warm Springs Creek via a bridge and goes on to Bear Mountain. The left fork continues up the creek and becomes noticeably narrower, implying that most of the traffic heads to Bear Mountain or just stops and turns around at this juncture.

About 3 miles in, there are a couple of switchbacks up and over a saddle with a short side trail off to the right.

A rocky talus slope across the creek marks the place to begin watching for the falls. As the trail passes a gray rock outcrop on the left, the entire falls complex comes into view. It is not tall, with maybe a 30-foot drop at the highest falls, but it is long. There is a left turn in the creek's path and a whole run of smaller drops with a big pool at the bottom. It is a nice falls, and well worth the walk.

Connections: Although the forest service map shows this trail connecting with the trail to Lost Knife Meadows, note the story in the User's Guide about the woman I met on this trail who'd had some difficulty finding trails in that area.

Why: A short, easy, informative leg-stretcher suitable for everyone.

Ease: Easy 1.2-mile circle with little elevation change once past the stairs up from the parking lot.

Season: Early June through October.

Maps: CWNF Visitor Map; USGS Bear Mountain, Idaho.

Information: Powell Ranger District, CWNF, 208-942-3113.

Trailhead: On the right at mileposts 148–149 on Highway 12.

The Hike: The mineral lick at Colgate Licks has been used by elk and other game for hundreds of years. The ancient Nez Perce had an access trail to the licks that came down the ridge at today's Jerry Johnson campground, then continued downriver. Johnson built a cabin on that trail, giving him convenient access to the old Nez Perce trail, the mineral lick, and the hot springs that now bear his name. The Carlin hunting party also used this lick

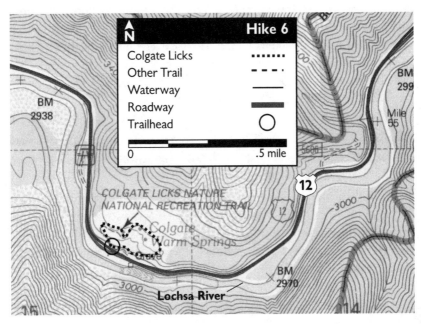

for hunting, and when the first downriver trail was built along the Lochsa River, it went right through the lick.

The licks are named for George Colgate, the cook for the 1893 Carlin hunting party of five: Colgate, guide Martin Spencer, and hunters William Carlin, Abraham Himmelwright, and John Pierce.

Although Spencer had taken a party over the same route the previous fall, he and the others were inexperienced in the Bitterroot Mountains, where heavy fall snows are possible. The three hunters traveled by train to Kendrick, Idaho, where they joined with the guide and cook, made final arrangements, and headed for the Lolo Trail. At Brown's Creek, near Weippe, Idaho, where they camped for the last time near "civilization," they were warned that they might have problems with snow because of their late start. They ignored the warning and headed east over the old Lolo Trail, then down the ridge via the old Nez Perce Trail. They arrived at Johnson's cabin on September 26, where they found Johnson, his partner Ben Keeley, and two hunters who were preparing to return to Missoula, Montana.

The party first learned that Colgate was not well when they arrived at the Lochsa. He was exhausted, and his feet and legs were swollen. Shortly thereafter, they learned that he had used a catheter for years but had not brought it with him on the trip.

The party continued their hunt until the morning of October 10, when they decided that the hunt had been successful enough and headed back over the Lolo Trail. They soon encountered three-foot-deep snow, and more was falling. Colgate was in serious condition, and there was concern about whether the horses could make the trip back. The men thought that they, but not Colgate, might make Musselshell Creek if they used snowshoes. But rather than abandon Colgate, they returned to the Lochsa River and began to build a raft.

Carlin returned to Johnson's cabin and persuaded Keeley to sell his share of the grub at the cabin for $250. He also persuaded Keeley to help build rafts and to accompany them down the river, and he bartered with Johnson for sugar, leaving him all the horses.

Colgate began to fail rapidly, with severe swelling in his limbs and fluid in his lungs. On November 2, one of his legs burst and discharged fluid, which improved his condition. Nonetheless, all agreed that he could not survive any journey out except by raft, and they started their trip down the Lochsa the next day.

The journey was difficult, and they had to portage the rafts around rapids many times. By November 9, Colgate was so stiff and cold that he could not walk, and by November 13, the rest of the party knew that if they were to survive they would have to abandon both Colgate and the rafts. They made Colgate comfortable and left him with what he might need for the remainder of his life.

The four men struggled on through the most difficult part of their journey. There was no trail along the Lochsa, and many times they had to hike up over cliffs and ridge points, then back down to the river. By November 21, they were too weak to walk for lack of food, and Himmelwright said that he had no control over his arms. They were lucky, for they soon met a rescue party headed upriver looking for them.

After their rescue, the men were criticized for their abandonment of Colgate. Once the initial furor died down, however, they were vindicated. The public realized that Colgate could not have lived long enough to get medical help and that staying with him would have meant death for all of the men.

The following year, an army expedition led by Lieutenant Elliott traveled the Jerry Johnson Trail down to the river to look for Colgate. They finally found some of his remains about 8 miles from where he had been left, his body carried downriver by the spring runoff of the Lochsa. They returned his remains to the flat area at the lower hot springs, today's Colgate Licks, and buried them.

My favorite part of this hike comes about $3/4$ of the way through, at the mineral lick. It's a muddy spot with rocks, and the trail through it is stepping stones. While walking the stones it's difficult to miss the multitude of game trails and tracks, abundant evidence of how the area is and has been used by the animals that live nearby. Steve remembers this spot from a hunting trip when he was twelve and thought it looked like a promising spot to find elk. It's a good spot to sort out the tracks belonging to the various local ungulates: deer, elk, and moose.

This trail is circular, well-worn, and easy to follow, with an assortment of informative signs along the way—about the Lochsa River, lodgepole pine, fire, the licks, and the pocket gopher. The trail travels through wooded areas, through the licks, past a group of old, gray, downed trees and roots, and through an open grassy meadow—a nice variety for such a short hike. There are even views of the Lochsa River and the breaks across it that head up into the Selway Bitterroot Wilderness. It's an excellent reason to get out of the car and walk for a half hour or so. Take a snack; there's a bench to sit on, with a view overlooking the Lochsa.

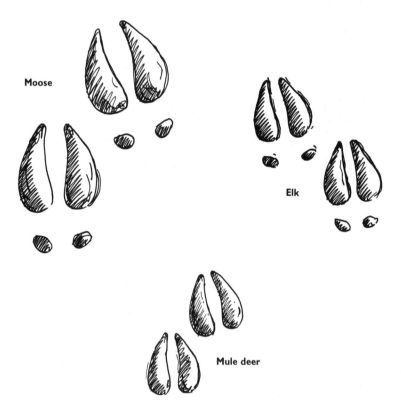

Moose

Elk

Mule deer

Why: Serpentine falls, wildflowers in season, and the shortest route be-tween Highway 12 and the Lolo Motorway.

Ease: Strenuous, with a 3,900-foot elevation gain for the entire $5\frac{1}{2}$ miles of trail, or 1,100 feet up for the mile-plus to the falls.

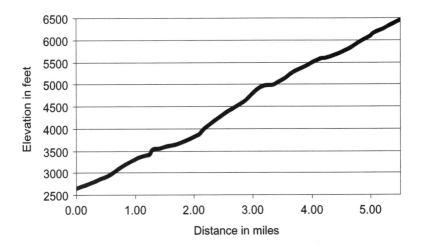

Season: Early June through October from the highway; mid-July through late September from the Motorway.

Maps: CWNF Visitor Map; USGS Holly Creek, Idaho.

Information: Powell Ranger District, CWNF, 208-942-3113.

Trailheads: The Highway 12 trailhead is between mileposts 135 and 136, a few yards downriver from the Eagle Pack Bridge parking area. The Motorway trailhead is on the left at mile 42.4 on the Motorway.

The Hike: The falls make the first mile or so of the trail up from the high-way worth hiking. They are in a chute, a place where the creek is forced down a gently bending and narrow rock corridor. There are also a good variety of wildflowers in season—primarily in this same lower section of the trail—more than 40 different types during a late June hike. And there is the possibility of wildlife, for I saw the tracks of moose, elk, coyote, and bear, as

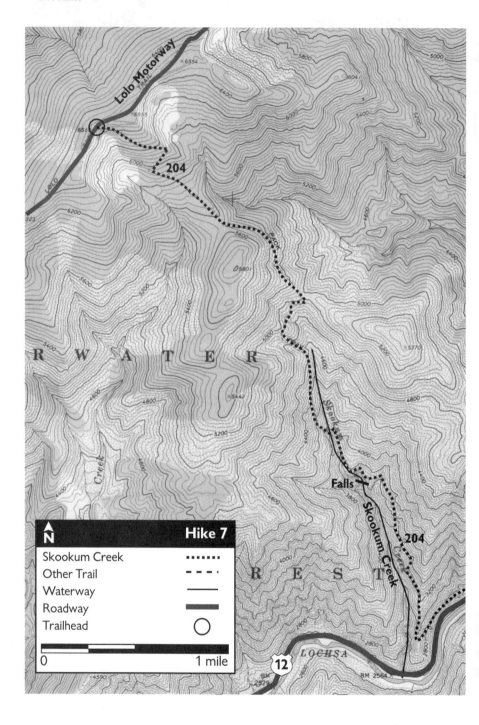

well as a rodent skull and a live snake.

From the top, there are some views of the Selway Crags and the Bitterroot Divide. Beyond these, the hike is just a hike—good exercise, for sure. But the trail is not well used, a bit hard to follow in one spot, and decidedly steep in several others.

From Highway 12, the trail heads downstream above the highway and river, paralleling them for about ⅓ mile, to a saddle on the ridge that separates the trailhead from the Skookum Creek drainage. On the saddle, there are fine views up the Lochsa, and the rock pinnacle above and behind the trail is worth a look. There is a side trail to the left that heads farther out onto the ridge corner, providing even better views.

As with most of the hike until the falls, this first section is in the open and could be hot, depending on the time of day and season. Besides the wildflowers and views of the close breaks across the Lochsa, there are some interesting rock outcroppings after the trail turns the corner and heads up Skookum Creek, including one that makes a good sitting spot for a snack, water, and view up the creek.

Most of the drainages are small until just before the falls, and the latter are visible from the second deep drainage that the trail traces. The falls are heard before they are seen. Because the viewing area is narrow, check for the falls soon after the first small rush of sound. The falls are small and confined, in a spot where the creek makes a sudden left turn behind a rock wall. The trail makes the same left turn, but not until the falls are out of view.

This section from trailhead to falls is the most gently and uniformly graded part of this trail and is the easiest walking. After the falls, the trail turns right and continues along the creek and into the trees, finally providing a bit of welcome shade.

There is a faint trail off to left and down to the creek a short distance after the turn, but it is not the main trail, and it is not heading down to the creek crossing that is on the map. Continue on with the creek on the left, even though the trail gets pretty skunky—

Various *Lomatia* species, otherwise known as the desert-parslies, are common in dry places. They vary from 10 to 60 inches tall and have fernlike, usually aromatic, leaves that are primarily basal. The flowers are most often yellow and borne in an umbel above the foliage.

Lomatiums have been an important food source for Native Americans. The roots usually were dug in the spring and were eaten raw or cooked, or they were dried to make a meal or flour. One species has the common name "biscuitroot." The leaves and flowers of another species were used to flavor meats, stews, and salads, and to make a tea for sore throats or colds.

Lewis and Clark noted in the journals that the roots of one were ground into a meal that was then shaped into flat cakes and carried from place to place. They also mentioned several times trading beads, buttons, and trinkets for "cous" roots or cakes.

Lomatia, however, are in the same family as the poison or water hemlock (*Cicuta douglasii*), and it is suggested that no members of this plant family should be eaten.

The plant is an important forage for deer, elk, antelope, and rodents, and the roots are eaten by pocket gophers, mice, and bear.

The word *lomatium* comes from the Greek *loma*, or border, and refers to the wings on the seeds of most species.

steep in spots, washed out in spots, overgrown in spots. There is a natural crossing spot near the end of the drainage, with a couple of four- to five-foot cedars to mark the spot.

After the crossing, it's uphill, uphill, uphill, through woods and several open areas. In some of the latter it can be difficult to see the trail. In a large meadow about 2 miles in, I couldn't see where it went but finally found the trail to the left of the group of three trees (two live, one dead), heading up the hill behind them.

About halfway up to the Motorway, there is a saddle. It makes a good stopping spot if you're not planning to hike all the way up. The trail is quite steep for the next quarter mile or so, and there are no views.

Hiking from the Motorway, the trail heads off to the left of the trailhead sign and into the open space between the trees, looking as though it's heading off the end of the world. It's not quite that bad, though the trail does head downhill without pause for essentially all of its 1,500-foot drop to the saddle between the Lost Creek and Skookum Creek drainages. The best views are from near the top—the Selway Crags can be seen from an angle that shows off Stanley Butte in front of them. The next view is a quick peek at the Bitterroot Divide as the trail turns right about $^3/_4$ mile later, and further down the trail there are openings through a couple of brief areas at the head of the Stanley Creek drainage.

At the fork in the trail about $1^1/_4$ miles in, take the left, around the left side of the knoll as is indicated on the map, and continue down.

Skookum means good or big in Chinook, making it a hard name to put together with this creek.

Why: A gorgeous meadow just beyond the Motorway trailhead, with wild-flowers in season, close views of Sherman Peak and the ridge that extends from it down toward the Lochsa River, and views across the river of Lochsa and Cantaloupe Peaks, and more. This also is the easiest through-hike between Highway 12 and the Motorway.

Ease: Moderate or strenuous, depending on how far you hike. There is less than a 1,000-foot elevation change over the first 3 miles of trail hiked from the Motorway down toward the Lochsa River. But since the trail continues down to the Lochsa for a total of 7½ miles and a 3,800-foot elevation drop, the hike can become strenuous.

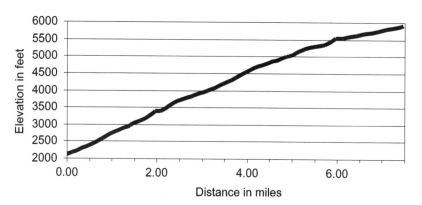

Season: June through October from Highway 12; mid-July through late September from the Motorway.

Maps: CWNF Visitor Map; USGS maps Liz Butte, Idaho, and Huckleberry Butte, Idaho.

Information: Lochsa Ranger District, CWNF, 208-926-4274.

Trailheads: The Highway 12 trailhead is at milepost 122–123. Turn into the road, immediately turn left, and head uphill into the small parking area, which contains the trailhead. The Motorway trailhead is on the left in No-see-um Meadow at mile 49.6 on the Motorway. Park there and walk down the short side road to the trailhead sign.

The camas (*Camassia quamash*) is a lily, lives in wet meadows, and blooms between mid-April and mid-June, depending on elevation. Its bright blue, star-shaped flowers are arranged in a spiky raceme at the top of 1- to 2-foot-tall stalks. The base of the stalk is surrounded by grasslike leaves.

Camas bulbs were a staple food and the primary vegetable eaten by northwest Native Americans, trappers, early settlers, and Lewis and Clark. The latter used it extensively, though they had some difficulty digesting it when they first added it to their diets. The bulb is best eaten during the fall. Traditionally, it was pit roasted, but now it often is boiled. The cooked bulb tastes somewhat like potatoes, but is less mealy and maybe a bit slimy.

In Lewis' journal entry of June 12, 1806, he says, "The quawmash is now in blume and from the colour of its bloom at a short distance it resembles lakes of fine clear water, so complete in this deseption that on first sight I could have sworn it was water."

Note: No-see-um Meadow was on the old Lolo Trail. It was not a popular camping place due to the bugs that are there even in mid-August, when most of the rest of the trail is relatively bugfree.

The Hike: This is a pleasant hike from either trailhead, even given the considerable elevation change; the meadow at the top and the views of Sherman Peak are what make it special. The views while hiking up from Highway 12 include Lochsa and Cantaloupe Peaks across the Lochsa River, with Old Man Point behind them.

The trail traces the contours along the side of the unnamed ridge between Sherman and No-see-um Creeks and follows Sherman Creek from end to end. Some sections of it pass through open brush fields or rocky areas, and some sections pass under the trees. There are a variety of tributary creeks to cross, the amount of water in each depending both on season and individual creek. The trail is quite worn in places, especially near the top, where it is deep with a shallow parallel tread that obviously has been used for walking. It is overgrown with brush in other places, especially the first 1/4 mile up from the highway trailhead.

Hiking from Highway 12 is amazingly easy. The trail starts at the right of the trailhead sign, while the Downriver Trail (hike 9) heads off to the left. It's extremely well-graded, and the elevation gain seems effortless. There are fine views once enough altitude has been gained of the two already-mentioned peaks across the Lochsa. The saddle between them is the first destination on the hike up Lochsa Peak (hike 11). From two miles up the trail it's possible to see Old Man Point and some higher peaks to the southeast of Cantaloupe, and Sherman Creek itself is a pleasure whenever it's visible along the way. On a late April hike there were glacier lilies, trillium, violets, and a herd of elk. All helped to make up for the snow that made it necessary to stop hiking after just 2 to 3 miles and for not being able to see more.

Hiking from the Motorway trailhead, the trail passes through the trees behind the trailhead sign, then turns left and right to follow the right track of the two tracks heading down into the meadow. There is a campsite on the right near the start, which was complete with a lot of ready-to-use firewood in 2000. Within five minutes, there is a second campsite and a second trailhead sign, the latter indicating that the Lochsa River is 8 miles distant. The trail then turns right and crosses the small creek, becomes narrower, and continues downhill and farther into the meadow.

The meadow is huge and delightful. It's grassy at first, with a border of large, dark green subalpine fir. It's the kind of place that feels as though

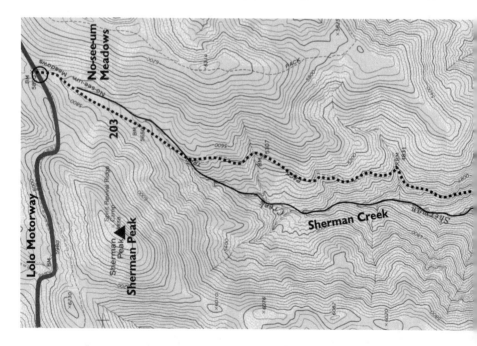

there must be animals hiding in the trees, waiting for the disturbance to pass so they can resume feeding. Unfortunately, the only animals I saw on this hike were winged and much too familiar: aggressive mosquitoes.

There was a sprinkling of wildflowers in the grass in late July that included red Indian paintbrush, pink spirea, and mountain bluebells—the latter blue, of course—and even a very late and lonely camas, also blue.

Traveling farther downhill through the meadow, the grass is gradually replaced by shrubs until eventually the trail leaves the meadow and enters a forest with a shrubby understory. It crosses Sherman Creek in $3/4$ mile, after which trees are less numerous. From between the trees, there's a great, close-as-you-can-get view of Sherman Peak just across the creek.

Even farther along, there is more to see of the ridge that extends from Sherman Peak toward the Lochsa River. The open meadows below its top probably mirror the one the trail traveled through at the start of the hike. The views down the creek include the heavily treed slopes of Lochsa and Cantaloupe Peaks across the Lochsa. After about three miles, the trail passes through an open area filled with mountain bluebells, then crosses the largest of the tributary creeks. That creek has several yards of rocky falls and chutes

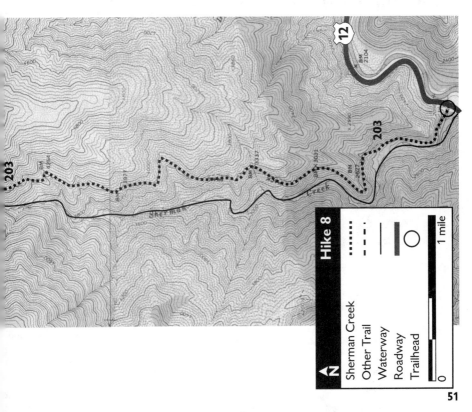

below it, and if hiked early in the spring from the Highway 12 trailhead, could take a bit of time to find a comfortable and dry crossing spot.

The trail splits on the downhill side of the crossing. The fork that turns right and continues along parallel to the falls and chutes is the trail along Sherman Creek. (The more or less straight ahead one is an outfitters trail to the No-see-um Butte area.) It is here, when hiking uphill, that it becomes obvious how far up in elevation the trail has come. Lochsa Peak, elevation 4,885, is now well below where you stand.

Continuing on down the hill, there are more streams to cross, one with a small waterfall, another with a wooden bridge. There are glimpses of Sherman Creek on occasion, and in general, a pleasant downhill hike of relatively moderate grade, given the elevation drop. Depending on the season and varying with elevation, there should be a wide variety of wildflowers in bloom.

Connections: At the highway, this trail shares a trailhead and parking space with the Downriver Trail (hike 9).

Note: It's sad but true that motorized vehicles are driven in places they are not allowed, and one of those places is No-see-um Meadow. When I visited in the year 2000, it looked fine, but I was told shortly thereafter that someone had driven a truck through it. This kind of misuse does more than spoil the view. It damages plants and small animals, compacts the soil, and the noise of the machines stresses the animals.

Meadows always look grassy to me, but what's growing in them isn't always grass, especially if the meadow is wet. A short rhyme might help you decide what's out there, even though it's probably not 100 percent accurate: Sedges have edges, rushes are round. Grasses are hollow from stem to ground.

Why: Easy access from Highway 12 to four contiguous sections of trail. Some feature picturesque drainages with falls and pools, while others have views of the Lochsa River and the foothills of the Selway-Bitterroot Wilderness.

Ease: Easy to moderate, depending on which section is hiked. The total length is 16 miles, with a total net elevation change of less than 350 feet.

Season: May through October, though it undoubtedly is available earlier and later, respectively, most years.

Maps: CWNF Visitor Map; USGS Huckleberry Butte, Idaho, McLendon Butte, Idaho, and Coolwater Mountain, Idaho.

Information: Lochsa Ranger District, CWNF, 208-926-4274. The Lochsa Historical Ranger Station is open daily between Memorial Day and Labor Day, from 9 a.m. to 5 p.m. 208-926-4275.

Trailheads: There are trailheads on Highway 12 at Sherman Creek, mileposts 122–123; the Lochsa Historical Ranger Station, mileposts 121–122; Fish Creek, mileposts 120–121; Beaver Flat, mileposts 117–118; the trail to Snowshoe Falls, mileposts 117–118; and Split Creek, mileposts 111–112.

The Hike:

The buildings of the Lochsa Historical Ranger Station were in place well before 1952, which was the year the highway reached the station. The first structure was built as a commissary in 1927. An office, tool room, and kitchen were added later, and that entire complex now is called the Combination Building. Other buildings were added as needed, and two of them were moved here, including the Boulder Creek Cabin, which was the first headquarters for the ranger district. Originally built at Boulder Flat, one mile upriver, it was dismantled and the logs floated downriver to the present site in 1926, where it was reassembled for use as a bunkhouse.

Prior to the completion of the highway to the station, all supplies were packed in along the Downriver Trail on the backs of horses or mules. The desk in the office of the Combination Building was packed in on a mule, balanced with a large ham and two bales of hay. It must have been a very large ham.

The 1934 Pete King Burn came close to destroying the entire

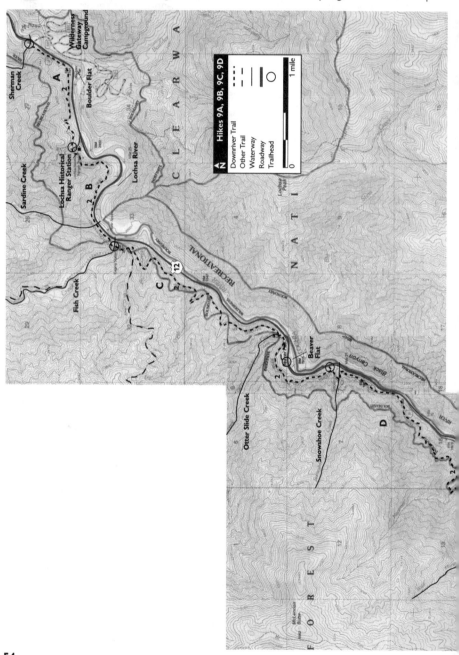

station, but the two hundred-plus men who were there, a water pumper, and bucket brigades saved all but a hay shed and corral. The heat was so intense, according to Louis Hartig, former Lochsa District Ranger, that several sections of the water-filled hose running from the pumper to the buildings were turned to ash and had to be replaced.

The Lochsa Historical Trail loosely parallels Highway 12 and the Lochsa River for about 16 miles. It is one of the few trails where, if possible, it makes sense to leave a car at each end of the trail and to walk in just one direction.

In general, the trail traces the curves of the breaks that line the highway side of the Lochsa River. Along the way it is possible to hear the river in places, see it in others, and to hear traffic in places, see it in others. Though there are some stretches where the grade seems steep, essentially all the ups and downs are short.

The trail spends more time in the open than in the trees, depending primarily on the orientation of the trail section. If the trail is south facing, it is open; if it is north facing, trees will be present. There are steep drop-offs on the highway side, but they almost always are masked by small trees and shrubs.

All sections have a good variety of wildflowers in season, but by early summer, which is June for this trail, the trail can become hot and overgrown with brush.

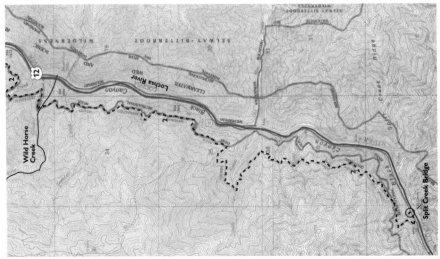

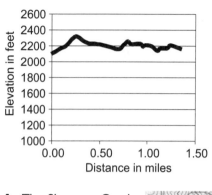

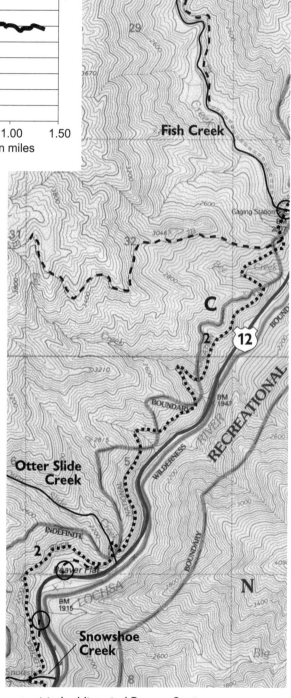

Fish Creek

Otter Slide
Creek

Snowshoe
Creek

A. The Sherman Creek to Lochsa Historical Ranger Station section is 1½ miles long. It starts by heading uphill into the woods, then spends most of its time in the open on a relatively level grade. Occasional big ponderosa pines with their orangy, puzzle-piece trunks stand out above the trail, and there are good views of Boulder Creek, the Lochsa, Fish Butte, and the saddle between Lochsa Peak and Cantaloupe Peak. There are two deep draws just before the trail reaches the ranger station, then a large, bare dirt spot on the downhill side of the trail. The dirt spot is a salt lick, and many game trails converge on it. Take the low fork shortly thereafter, even though it may be overgrown, to continue on the trail, or to head down to visit the Historical Ranger Station.

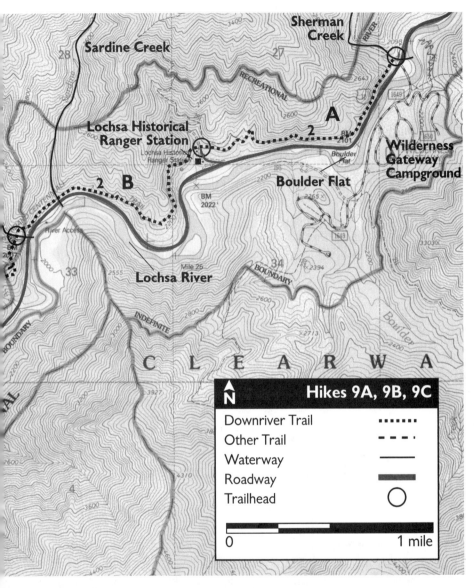

B. The Historical Ranger Station to Fish Creek section starts uphill, on the left side of a gravel road that is above the ranger station's main visitor building. The trailhead sign there states that Fish Creek is 2 miles downriver, but it's the shortest 2 miles I've ever had the pleasure of hiking. (It's actually closer to 1½ miles long, which is good because this is my least favorite section of the trail).

As the trail leaves the ranger station area, it crosses a small creek lined with cedars. Take the right fork at the barbed wire fence, which the trail will parallel as it heads uphill through woods. Once the trail breaks out into the open, there are views of the river and of Fish Butte, and of a fine rock outcrop below the trail. Then the trail heads down to highway level and is next to the road for about 100 yards, passing the sign for the Fish Creek Trailhead before heading back into the woods shortly thereafter. Another 100 yards or so is spent just inside the woods at the same level until the trail is directly across from the Lochsa River access area on the other side of the highway. At this point it crosses Sardine Creek. Then it heads back up and into the high brush until the trailhead sign, which is oddly located some feet above the road along Fish Creek. Either plunge down the hill via a few switchbacks to a spot directly across from the bridge that crosses the creek just off of Fish Creek Road, or continue straight ahead down to the road, reaching it across from a dirt pullout. The latter appears to be used more often and is a bit better walking. Neither is marked at Fish Creek Road.

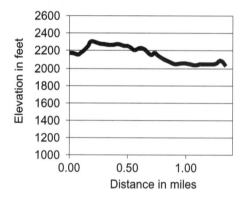

C. The Fish Creek section to either Beaver Flat or Snowshoe Falls is 4 miles long, according to the signs, and starts at the bridge across Fish Creek. It heads uphill through the woods to a signed fork where the trail to Fish Butte (hike 14), continues uphill to the right. The downriver trail heads downhill on the left fork even though the sign has just one arrow (pointing uphill) and seems to suggest both trails head that way.

There are several sections overgrown primarily with ferns and thimbleberry in this part of the hike. On a fall morning, the dew can be damp enough to soak your pant legs through within a short distance. At any time of year, the overgrowth means pushing against and tripping over vegetation, having shoelaces untied by it, and sometimes not being able to see the trail tread. But this section travels through the best drainages, making it well worth the effort. Assuming my creek identifications are correct, Otter Slide Creek is

Bunchberry (*Cornus canadensis*) is that low-to-the-ground plant you see that looks like a twig from a dogwood tree. It looks that way because it is a member of the dogwood family. It has the same single, white flower that the trees do, but the eye-catching white "petals" are actually four large, white modified leaves (bracts) that sit beneath a cluster of tiny greenish-white to purplish flowers. The flowers become a bunch of red berries in the fall, hence the common name. The plant is 2 to 8 inches high and grows in patches in shady forests.

The berries are eaten raw by various Native Americans and are the favorite fall food of the ruffed grouse. The oval, evergreen leaves with parallel veins are eaten by white-tailed deer.

my favorite. It has a flat, gentle run of water sliding over slabs of rock and making pools. Snowshoe Creek has lovely falls that can be reached directly from the highway (hike 15), with a bridge to stand on while admiring the two streams of water that fall within the rock face of the hill, then come together at its base. Wildhorse Creek has a pool above the trail that flows two to three feet down over a rock face, and a waterfall below the trail.

About a half mile before Snowshoe Falls, the trail passes through a large, open, relatively flat area known as Beaver Flat. There is an old trail sign along it that pinpoints the start of the trail heading down into Beaver Flat.

Just before the Snowshoe Creek drainage, there is a trail to the left that goes down to Highway 12 at the three-part Wilderness Information sign and the Snowshoe Creek Falls trailhead. It's an easy left to miss, but if you reach the falls, you've passed it.

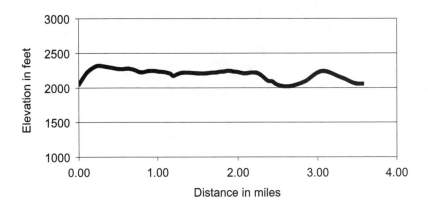

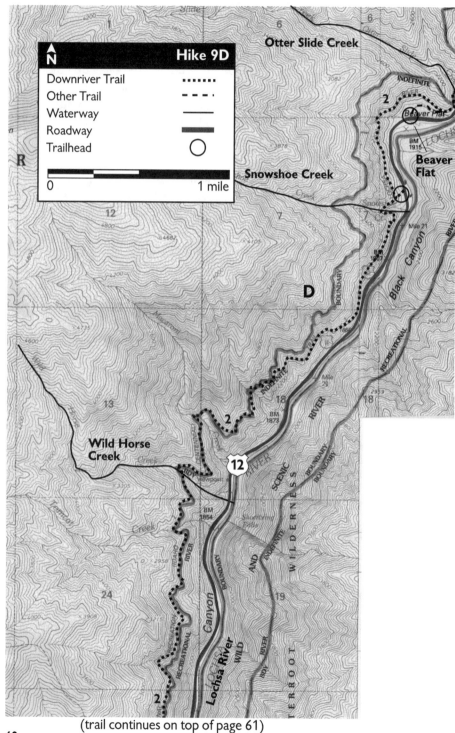

(trail continues on top of page 61)

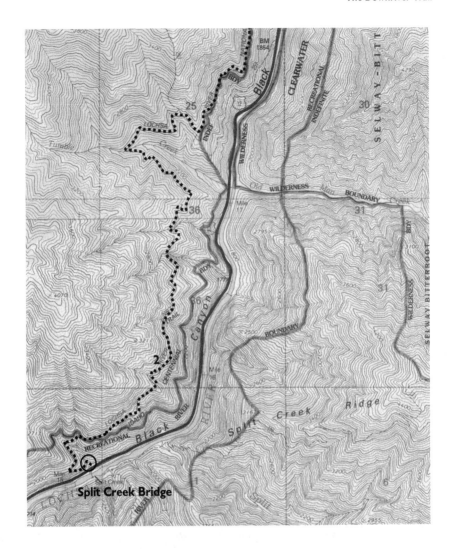

Split Creek Bridge

D. The longest section is from Snowshoe Falls or Beaver Flat to the Split Creek trailhead, above the Black Canyon of the Lochsa River. It's higher above the highway here than anywhere else along the trail, and once up on this long 7-plus mile section, there's no place to go but forward or back. While that's no problem while hiking the first half of the trail west from Snowshoe, the last half is another story. Not only does the tread get progressively poorer, but the ins and outs of what seem to be innumerable drainages give the impression that the trail is much longer than it is. I definitely had the feeling that many drainages had been added to the landscape after the map was made. On the other side of the river there are a couple of waterfalls to enjoy along this section.

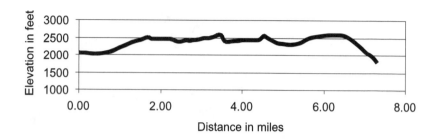

I had one of my more interesting hiking experiences near the middle of this section. While stepping over a small bit of creek, I caught movement out of the corner of my eye. I looked to the uphill side and saw a small black bear cub crossing the same creek. Seeing a bear cub close at hand is high on my list of things I don't want to see when out hiking because it usually means a mother bear is nearby. But having survived the encounter, I'm delighted to have seen the cub.

The Split Creek packbridge, then Split Creek, are visible near the end of the trail. But there is still another mile of trail to go, during which it traces the drainage that the packbridge is adjacent to, then switchbacks part way back along that stream before switchbacking down to the trailhead at Split Creek.

A note in passing: Although the entire 16 miles of the Downriver Trail is near the highway, there was more bear scat on it during one autumn hike than I've ever seen anywhere else.

Connections: The trails to Fish Butte (hike 14), up Fish Creek (hike 13), to Snowshoe Falls (hike 15), and up Sherman Creek (hike 8), all intersect with this trail.

Note: The Downriver Trail is part of the Idaho Centennial Trail.

Why: Moderate hike along a scenic creek drainage, plus a waterfall.

Ease: Moderate, with a 1,300-foot elevation gain over $4\frac{1}{2}$ miles to Huckleberry Flat.

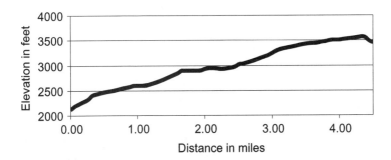

Season: Early June through October.

Maps: CWNF Visitor Map; USGS Huckleberry Butte, Idaho.

Information: Lochsa Ranger District, CWNF, 208-926-4274.

Trailhead: Turn into the Wilderness Gateway Campground, milepost 122–123 on Highway 12. Drive to the trailhead parking on the right, just past camping loop "C." Walk back along this road to the signed trailhead and the footbridge over Boulder Creek.

The Hike: Some bodies of water are well-named, and Boulder Creek is right up there on that list. When stream flows are low, it seems the creek is nothing but boulders. When stream flows are high in the spring and early summer, the boulders mean that not an ounce of its water isn't rapids or turbulence.

> I saw my first cougar tracks on this trail while hiking in December during the early 1990s. They weren't fresh, but they got my attention—as cougar tracks always do. I see them most often when cross-country skiing.
>
> Cougar are the largest of our wild cats and can weigh up to 200 pounds. They are largely nocturnal, though individual cats some-

times don't seem to be aware of that: Steve has encountered two at midday, and many others have seen cougar during daylight hours. I consider myself fortunate to have seen three—in the dark, and from inside a car. Cougar rarely cause problems for humans except at the human–cougar habitat interface, when they may consider small children or domestic animals as prey.

The worst of the uphill grades along the trail come at its start and are over not long after hiking the two initial switchbacks through the woods. Then the trail heads out into a brushfield, with good views of Lochsa and Cantaloupe Peaks on the opposite side of Boulder Creek, and of Fish Butte across the highway. Trees return gradually, Douglas fir and ponderosa pine coming first, until the trail is predominantly in the woods.

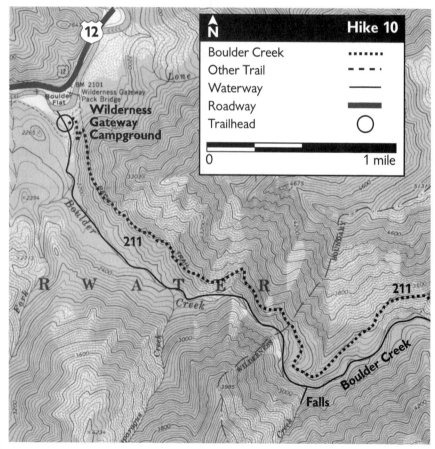

Some of the drainages traced by the trail are deep, and two rocky ones between 2 and 3 miles in are particularly nice. The first is almost a gorge, with sheer rock walls decorated with moss, shrubs, and small trees. The second has huge, smooth slabs of rock below the trail. Between the two are the best rock outcrops you'll see on the trail side of the creek.

The wilderness boundary is signed about 3 miles in. Shortly after, Cantaloupe Creek comes down to join Boulder Creek via a narrow waterfall that traces an S-shaped curve in several steps down the opposite hillside.

The trail junctions with two others at Huckleberry Flat about $4\frac{1}{2}$ miles in, at the edge of an open knoll with a good lunch spot under the ponderosa pines. Huckleberry and Cantaloupe Buttes are to the south and east.

The trail is generally in good shape with a hard, firm tread. Some sections were muddy in June and surely would be dusty later. Some sections are washboarded from the heavy horse traffic the trail gets during the fall hunting season.

Though the trail enters the wilderness and continues deep into it, the last time I hiked it I was reminded of just how difficult it is to "get away from it all." On a beautiful, clear June day, the sky was crisscrossed with contrails both fresh and fading.

Connections: At Huckleberry Flat, trail FS#221 goes to Stanley Hot Springs and on to connect with the trail to Lochsa Peak, FS#220 (hike 11) after 5 miles. Beware: There no longer is a bridge on that trail over Boulder Creek, and in high water the crossing could be more than interesting. Trail FS#247 goes from Huckleberry Flat to Gold Hill. The Boulder Creek Trail continues into the wilderness, to and beyond Fish Lake.

Why: Fine views of the ridge the Lolo Motorway follows from Rocky Ridge to past Castle Butte.

Ease: Strenuous, with a 3,000-foot elevation gain in about 3¾ miles, plus another few hundred feet up for the best, longer-range views toward Castle Butte.

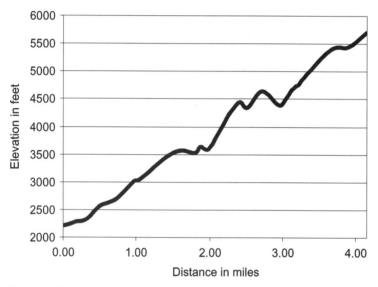

Season: Early June through October.

Maps: CWNF Visitor Map; USGS Huckleberry Butte, Idaho.

Information: Lochsa Ranger District, CWNF, 208-926-4274.

Trailhead: Turn into the Wilderness Gateway Campground, milepost 122–123 on Highway 12. Drive to the trailhead parking on the right, just past camping loop "C." Then either walk the road farther uphill until you see the wilderness and trailhead signs on your right, or cross the road and follow the trail that parallels the road to take you to the same signs. The saddle that is the hike's first destination is visible from the road to the trailhead, as is the slope to its left that should be climbed to get the best views.

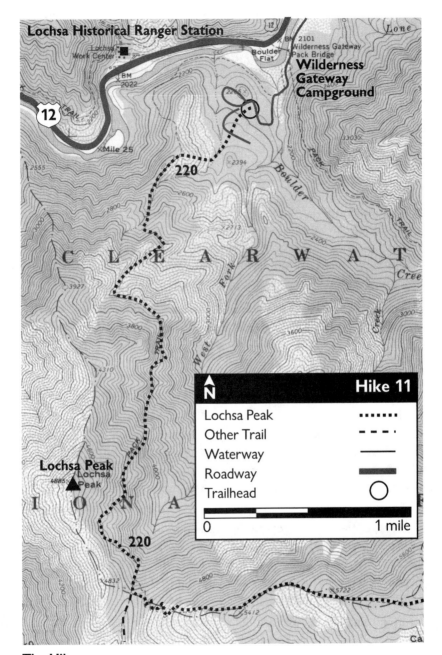

The Hike:

I led a hike up this trail only once, and most of the people with me that day consider it to be the hardest hike I've led. I don't agree, although I do remember that the day we hiked was exceptionally hot and the trail was more difficult than any of us expected. Also that we had to hike beyond the saddle, up the steepest part of the trail, to see the best views. But it was worth it; from there we had views that can't be seen from other hikes on this side of the Lochsa.

The trail starts gently, curving around a small creek and behaving as if uphill was the last place it was going. But not for long. Within a few hundred yards it starts up, and then there's no relief, no stretch where there are more than three level or downhill steps in a row except when the trail crosses bridges over creeks. The grade varies from gentle to a tad steep until the saddle. Beyond that, it's just plain steep—but worth the effort it takes.

From the saddle, just Castle and No-see-um Buttes are visible. From another 400 feet or so up, almost the whole sweep of the high country that Lewis and Clark traveled can be seen. From the left, there is Rocky Ridge, Bowl Butte, the Willow Creek drainage, Sherman Peak, No-see-um Butte, Bald Mountain with the Motorway visible as a slash across the front, Castle Butte with its lookout, and the Fish and Sherman Creek drainages. In the latter two, even a bit of each creek and the trail along it are visible.

From bottom to top, the trail traces the contours of Lochsa Peak, above the West Fork Boulder Creek drainage. It moves from treed areas, sometimes with cooling breezes, to open and very hot areas. There are times when the tracings seem excessive, when there seem to be innumerable drainages. But once the trail starts crossing wooden bridges, the end of the trail is near.

Most of the views from this hike are up the Boulder Creek drainage. Early on, the trail up its east side can be seen, and at various twists and turns, the Wilderness Gateway campground, Highway 12, and the Lochsa River. But the bottom line is that this trail is hiked for the views across the river. Save the local scenery for the trip back downhill to the trailhead.

Connections: This trail continues into the lake area and connects with trail FS#221 to Huckleberry Flat and FS#211 along Boulder Creek (hike 10). Check with the Forest Service before assuming that either of these connections is actually possible.

Wilderness Gateway Campground Trail FS#195

Why: Two short and easy walks, one of which goes to an overlook that provides a fine view of the Lochsa Historical Ranger Station.

Ease: Easy. Both are short with little elevation gain.

Season: Early June through October, possibly earlier, and depending on when the campground opens.

Maps: CWNF Visitor Map; USGS Huckleberry Butte, Idaho.

Information: Lochsa Ranger District, CWNF, 208-926-4274. The Lochsa Historical Ranger Station is open daily between Memorial Day and Labor Day, from 9 a.m. to 5 p.m. 208-926-4275.

Trailhead: Turn into the Wilderness Gateway Campground, milepost 122–123 on Highway 12. One trailhead is at the end of camping loop "C." The other section of trail has several entrances: one next to the bridge over the Lochsa, one each from camping loops "A" and "B," and one that coincides with the entrance to the amphitheater.

The Hike: These two short hikes are good as leg-stretchers or places to walk when camped at Wilderness Gateway rather than as destination hikes.

The trail out of camping loop "C" parallels the highway and river the whole way, and is a good, short walk with a nice sample of the local short understory plants: Solomon's seal, bunchberry, queencup, twin berry, thimbleberry, snowberry, penstemon, false lupine, vetch, self heal, and at least two different kinds of ferns. It starts by crossing a small stream, then stays level and comfortably wide through the trees for $1/4$ mile or so before heading uphill. There is a quick look at the Lochsa Historical Ranger Station before a short downhill, then a curve to the right and back upriver to the overlook. The overlook has short stone walls topped with wood and is directly across from the Ranger Station entrance.

The trail on the other end of Wilderness Gateway is most easily accessed from the small parking area by the amphitheater entrance. That section is paved and wheelchair accessible to the amphitheater, which is a few yards from its start. The trail continues from that point as a dirt path that circles behind camping loops "B" and then "A," with marked turnoffs for each. After crossing a stream, it heads along a hillside overlooking part of Wilderness Gateway, then on through a mostly deciduous woods of short trees and tall understory plants until it dead ends at the trail segment coming up from near the bridge.

The segment up from near the bridge also is the beginning of the trail that heads up to Lone Knob. It is steep but has a stream crossing near the bottom with an attractive pool and small falls.

Walking end to end on this campground trail is a trip of about 1 mile. Some of the tread isn't great, for it slopes to outside, can be narrow, and contains some very sturdy wood stubs left from cleared brush.

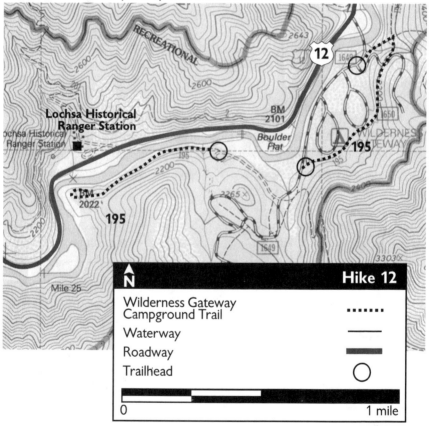

Connections: The trail up Lone Knob is a secondary trail and not frequently maintained. The USGS map shows the longer of these campground trails continuing past its junction with the trail to Lone Knob, but in 2000, it did not—at least not obviously. The trailheads for hikes 10 and 11 are also within the Wilderness Gateway Campground.

Self-heal (*Prunella vulgaris*) is one of the more common plants along the trails. It is usually just a few inches high, with oblong pointed leaves opposite each other and scattered along the stem. The usually purplish flowers are in a short spike at the top of the stem and looks a bit like a stretched-out clover. They appear between May and September.

Self-heal once was a commonly used medicinal herb, and it is still used to make tea. Traditionally, it was used to control internal and external bleeding. Some Native Americans used it to make tea for the heart, while others put its juice on boils. The leaves were placed on cuts, bruises, and other skin inflammations, or they were crushed and mixed with grease to be used as an ointment. Self-heal also was used to heal wounds caused by sharp tools, as is evidenced by another of its names, carpenter's herb.

The plant is found worldwide. The word *Prunella* comes from the German, meaning quinsy or angina, which it was used to cure. Tests have shown that there is no biochemical basis for the healing properties.

| # Fish Creek FS#2240

Why: Wildflowers in season, a beautiful creek, and one of the few relatively level hikes off Highway 12.

Ease: Moderate, with a 700-foot elevation gain in the 4$\frac{1}{2}$ miles to Obia Cabin at Hungery Creek.

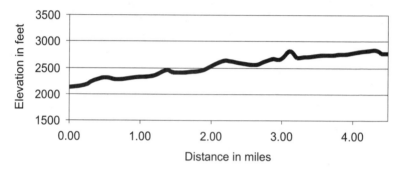

Season: Early June through October.

Maps: CWNF Visitor Map; USGS Huckleberry Butte, Idaho, and McLendon Butte, Idaho. Older CWNF Visitor Maps, some topographic maps, and the trailhead sign list this trail as #224.

Information: Lochsa Ranger District, CWNF, 208-926-4274.

Trailhead: Turn left on to the road along Fish Creek at milepost 120–121 on Highway 12. The trailhead is signed about a mile up that road, at a parking area with a pit toilet.

The Hike: Obia Cabin, at the junction of Fish and Hungery Creeks, was built in 1935. It replaced a log-and-split cedar shake cabin that had been built five years earlier but was destroyed in the 1934 Pete King Burn. Obia Cabin originally was used by maintenance crews, then for game counting, then again for trail and telephone line crews. The cabin was named for the creek's original name, Obia Creek. That name came from hunters, one apparently a Russian, who found two elk cows on the creek. The Russian called out, "I got Obia," meaning two. The creek's name was later changed to that given it by Clark in 1805, Hungery Creek. A branch of Hungery Creek currently is known as Obia Creek.

The flat field around the cabin makes a fine lunch spot, and the large boulders in Hungery Creek are suitable for sitting. I saw blue-eyed grass in the field, a flower that by itself was worth the hike, for I've not seen it elsewhere. Blue-eyed grass (*Sisyrinchium angustifolium*), is a member of the iris family. It has one to a few luminescent, pale blue, six-petaled flowers (actually, three are petals and three are sepals) that stand above the narrow, grasslike leaves. And luminescent is the right word, for the flower seems to glow.

This trail is like most river trails in that it has plenty of ups and downs along the way. It closely follows Fish Creek except when tracing side stream drainages or while on a shortcut it takes when the creek makes a horseshoe turn. The latter is where the only sustained elevation changes occur, though by comparison to other hikes off Highway 12, they hardly count.

There are wonderful rocks on this hike, samples of granite of the Bitterroot batholith. In the creek, there are small rocks, big rocks, and huge rocks. In one spot, a half mile or so in, the creek makes a wide turn and undercuts a rock wall. On the hike back out to the trailhead, a huge boulder is visible atop the wall.

Some of the rocks form gray cliffs above and below the trail, some with

There is a whole genus found only in the Northwest that is named for William Clark. He collected the first samples of the genus along the Clearwater River on the 1806 return trip.

The one that occurs in the area covered by this book is the beautiful or deerhorn Clarkia (*Clarkia pulchella*), and it has outstanding and quite elaborate flowers. They are bright pink to rose lavender in color and can be seen on dry sites from May to June. At times, whole hillsides along the Lochsa bloom with Clarkia, often accompanied by a few yellow sedums (*Sedum leibergii* or *Sedum stenopetalum*). The Clarkia's petals look like tiny oak leaves, except for the color, of course. Each has three narrow lobes and a small white stigma in the center. The leaves are narrow. And while this description may not seem adequate, the flowers are unmistakable.

The sedums are easier to describe. Sedums are a succulent, meaning fleshy and juicy, with starlike yellow flowers in branched clusters that sit a few inches above the foliage. *Sedum leibergii* blooms along the Lochsa and up the trails from it.

surfaces cracked into shapes not found in old-style geometry books, and with plants growing wherever they take roothold. The light-colored rock wall above the first stream crossing at Pondosa Creek, with its growth of moss and small plants, is particularly nice.

There is a bridge across Willow Creek about 3 miles in, and a fork in the trail soon after. Stay left, around the area where Willow joins Fish Creek, to continue. There is also a trail off to the left a few yards later that heads

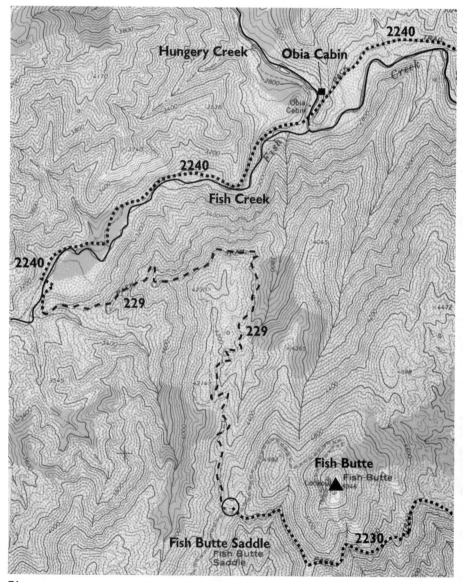

down to the creek, but the trail up Fish Creek continues straight ahead.

On one June hike up the creek, there were 31 different species of identifiable wildflowers, including the blue-eyed grass and an entire hillside covered with hot pink Clarkia. There also were ripe strawberries and huckleberries.

I'm told that steelhead spawn in Fish Creek, but I've not been there at the right time of year to see them. I did see bright orange crayfish once, another time a frog. The latter is alarmingly rare these days.

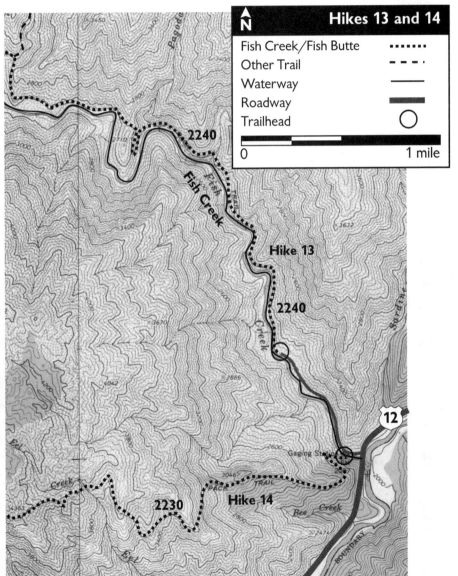

Hikes 13 and 14

Fish Creek/Fish Butte	•••••••
Other Trail	– – – ·
Waterway	——
Roadway	▬▬▬
Trailhead	◯

0   1 mile

The hike up Fish Creek is out in the open most of the way because the area burned in the same fire that destroyed the original Obia Cabin. The southern exposures not only make it hot to hike but also make it difficult for trees to return and grow to large size. The only shady spots are in low areas that have supported the growth of moderate-sized deciduous trees—alder, small maples, and birch.

Connections: When the water levels are low, this hike can be combined with the trail up Fish Butte (hike 14) for a 12-mile circle hike. See that hike for details. It is also possible to continue hiking along Fish Creek for at least a mile or two past Hungery Creek. I've done so once and remember it as a pleasant, level walk in the woods. The old trail up Hungery Creek is no longer maintained.

Snowbush (*Ceanothus velutinus*) is common on the open slopes above the Lochsa and elsewhere, and it is easy to identify. Its leaves are shiny, leathery, and dark green, with three prominent veins. The leaves are broadly elliptic in shape, and the plant is evergreen.

The bush gets its name from its small white flowers that bloom in pyramidal clusters along the sides of its branches, near the ends of the twigs. When in bloom, they look like patches of new snow.

Snowbush is one of the first species to return to an area after fire. Its seeds can lie dormant for up to two hundred years, their germination stimulated by fire. The plant also sprouts new growth from stems. Snowbush fixes nitrogen as do the more familiar beans and legumes. The roots convert atmospheric nitrogen into a form useful to plants via bacteria that live in nodules on their roots.

The entire plant is aromatic, and its flowers have a spicy scent. Native Americans used its leaves for tobacco and tea, and its roots to make a red dye. It is browsed by elk, deer, and moose and may be an important winter and early spring food for them.

The closely related redstem ceanothus (*C. sanguineus*) has the same ability to return after fire and to fix atmospheric nitrogen. Its leaves are not shiny, have three prominent veins, and are thin, deciduous, and a bit narrower than those of *C. velutinus*. The bark is reddish purple and the plant is a winter browse for elk and deer. Its flowers form tiny white clusters.

Many of the *Ceanothus* species contain saponin in the flowers. It is toxic but apparently not to the animals that eat the plants. The early settlers and Native Americans used the flowers as a substitute for soap.

Why: The best views from a Highway 12 hike of the Selway Crags, Chimney Peak, Coolwater Ridge, and the Selway-Bitterroot Wilderness high country.

Ease: Strenuous, with a 2,600-foot elevation gain in about 4½ miles to the saddle southeast of the butte. See map with hike 13.

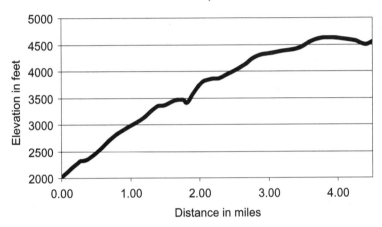

Season: Early June through October.

Maps: CWNF Visitor Map; USGS Huckleberry Butte, Idaho, and McLendon Butte, Idaho. Older CWNF Visitor Maps, some topographic maps, and the trailhead sign list this trail as #223.

Information: Lochsa Ranger District, CWNF, 208-926-4274.

Trailhead: Turn left on to the road along Fish Creek at milepost 120–121 on Highway 12. The signed trailhead for this trail and the Downriver Trail is a few yards later on the left, at the bridge over Fish Creek. (See pages 74–75 for map.)

The Hike:

> Both times I've hiked up Fish Butte I've seen the same wildlife: vultures. And this is the only hike in the area where I've seen them. It makes me wonder what they know about hiking this trail that I don't.

The first time there were six or eight of them riding the thermals above a large draw that holds a couple of enormous, free-standing boulders. There were vultures on the boulders, too, sunning themselves, perhaps, or just resting. The second time, I saw vultures in the air, just a couple.

Vultures are about as lovely a bird to watch in the air as you can see, seeming to float effortlessly. They're easily recognizable, too. First, there's the shape they take when flying. It's called "dihedral," and what that means is they hold their wings in a shallow, V-shape profile. Second, their wings are distinctive in that the shoulder, or epaulette part, is black, while the rest of the wing is pale gray. Last, if they get close enough or the sun hits them just right, you can see there are no feathers on their heads.

On the first hike, my hiking buddy said "It's nice to see vultures. It means that things are being taken care of." I agree, no matter what it is that means.

The trail to Fish Butte shares tread with the Downriver Trail (hike 9) for the first half mile. During that time, it heads up through the woods and along Fish Creek, then turns to follow the Lochsa River. This may well be the longest stretch of shade in the entire hike, depending, of course, on the time of day. Much of the rest is through the brush fields that are the result of the 1934 Pete King Burn. Trees have a difficult time getting started and growing on these south-facing slopes. It is no place to be hiking during midday in July or August.

At the lower elevations of the hike, the shrub fields are punctuated by an occasional charred snag or tall ponderosa pine. Most of the other trees are in the draws with more hospitable north- or east-facing areas. There is also a lot of bracken fern.

The granite rocks along the trail are immense, in all shades of gray, rounded and smoothed by the passage of time. They can be in flat slabs, jumbled piles, or steeply rising rock walls. Sometimes they are huge boulders like the vultures' rocks, and in another spot they are piled one on top of another, looking like a giant cairn for near-sighted hikers.

The views begin about 1 1/2 miles into the hike. First, there is part of Coolwater Ridge, a not-very-imposing treed stretch with a bit of a rocky top. More and more of it becomes visible as the hike progresses, eventually the whole stretch from Andy's Hump to Roundtop can be seen. This ridge may not look like much, but it is nearly inaccessible without hiking up between 3,600 and 5,200 feet. The road up to and along its top is driveable only by full-sized four-wheel-drive vehicles, and then only barely. I've been up twice, in other people's vehicles, to hike trails to two fine places: the Selway-Bitterroot area near Chimney Peak and the Selway Crags, and along Glover Ridge.

As the trail climbs farther up Fish Butte, the snow-topped, rocky Selway Crags and Chimney Peak become visible, as well as the ridge that connects the latter with Coolwater. That ridge includes the interestingly named Louse Point, which sits high above the equally interestingly named Louse Lake. By the time the trail reaches the saddle that separates the Lochsa side from the Fish Creek side of Fish Butte, there is as good a view of that area as is possible to see by hiking—except, of course, from the lookout site on top of the Butte. I've not yet hiked that. Some days there actually is a limit to how far uphill I will walk.

Connections: With USGS maps and a chat with the Forest Service in advance, it is possible to put together a circle hike that combines this trail with that along Fish Creek (hike 13). Continue on the trail around Fish Butte, where you will cross the road that leads to the top of the butte, and drop down and across a small clearing to walk down the back of the butte on an old fire road, trail FS#229. It ends at Fish Creek. Rock hop or wade across to pick up the trail along Fish Creek. It is about 2 miles from there to Obia Cabin, Hungery Creek, and the connection with the Fish Creek Trail.

As of 2000, the sign at the separation of this trail and the Downriver Trail has just one arrow, pointing up the hill. The latter trail actually goes to the left and downhill, while this trail heads uphill as the arrow suggests.

Note: I did drive up to the top of Fish Butte once. While there, I spent all my time enjoying the views in the other direction—toward the Motorway, primarily up the Willow Creek drainage and over toward the ridge down from Sherman Peak.

Why: A lovely falls just a brisk and short ¹/₂ mile or so from the highway.

Ease: Easy, but with a stiff uphill at the start.

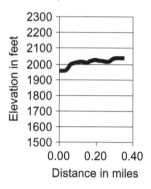

Season: Early June through October.

Maps: CWNF Visitor Map; USGS Huckleberry Butte, Idaho. (Neither shows the bit of trail from the highway in to the Downriver Trail.)

Information: Lochsa Ranger District, CWNF, 208-926-4274.

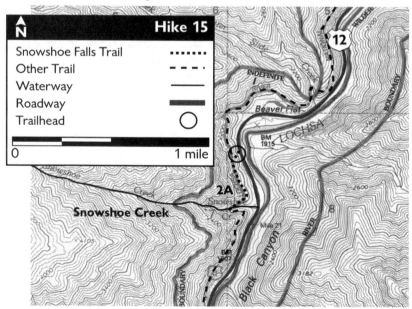

Trailhead: Mileposts 117–118 on Highway 12.

The Hike: The waterfall is worth the uphill at the start of this short hike. As the water flows down over and between rock walls, it splits into more than one stream, which reconnect just before touching bottom. There is a wood bridge crossing the creek just below the falls that provides a fine photo opportunity.

The worst part of this hike is the start: a steep uphill off the highway, then a few steep but short switchbacks. Once past the bright green, moss-covered, and wet corner with the barest remains of a tree trunk on the left, however, the uphill is much more gentle.

This trail joins the Downriver Trail about halfway to the falls, at which point the trail turns to the right, heads away from the highway, and leaves the trees as it follows Snowshoe Creek back to the falls. The walking is level then, and downhill as the trail approaches the falls.

Even on this short walk, there is a nice variety of wildflowers in season, including some personal favorites: bunchberry, queencup, and wild ginger. There is also a good variety of ferns.

Connections: This trail is one entryway to the Downriver Trail (hike 9). Turn right at that junction to head upriver toward Fish Creek, the Lochsa Historical Ranger Station, and Sherman Creek. Turn left and keep walking past Snowshoe Creek to head downriver toward Split Creek.

Wild ginger (*Asarum caudatum*) is a low-growing, evergreen plant with dark green, slightly shiny, heart-shaped leaves. It grows in moist spots in the shade, sometimes in fairly big patches.

Ginger has the most unusual, even bizarre, flower imaginable. It is purple brown and bell like, with three widely spread sections that fold backward. Each ends in a long point like a tendril, and each has a white spot at its base. Ginger flowers between April and July, though you will have to look under the leaves to see them. I would never have seen one if a friend had not pointed it out. Since then, I have enjoyed showing the flower to many others, and all have been as surprised and delighted as I was.

The leaves have a lemon-ginger smell if crushed. Native Americans used the leaves as a poultice and the rhizomes to make a drink to aid indigestion, colds, and the flu.

Why: Short walk into a narrow canyon with seasonal flowers, moss and fern-draped rock walls, and innumerable small falls and pools.

Ease: Easy, with a gentle but consistently uphill grade over a mile or so of trail that is in good to poor condition.

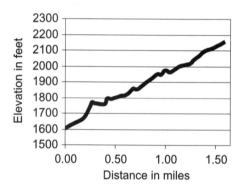

Season: April through November.

Maps: CWNF Visitor Map; USGS Lowell, Idaho.

Information: Lochsa Ranger District, CWNF, 208-926-4274.

Trailhead: Turn right at mileposts 103–104 on Highway 12, on to the road along Canyon Creek. The trailhead is signed, about $\frac{1}{10}$ of a mile in.

The Hike: When I hiked this trail in June, I thought it just a good leg-stretcher for after breakfast or an early dinner if camped nearby, or as a break in a driving day. After hiking it in April, I changed my mind. The difference? Though it's a short hike, the beauty along the trail make this more than just exercise.

In April there was no brush overhanging the trail, and the trail was decorated with huge masses of three lovely wildflowers: white trillium, yellow glacier lilies, and violet purple mountain kittentails. (Note: The yellow glacier lily is also known as dogtooth violet, adder's-tongue, snow lily, and pale fawn lily.) With the higher April water flow, the creek was picturesque, either running over rocks and making short waterfalls or collecting in small pools preparing to head down over the next falls.

The trail heads out of the parking lot area along the creek. For the first mile or so, it never strays far from that bit of water, and is either at creek level or a short bit above it.

There is a sign for trail FS#207 on the left in the first small clearing, a trail that is not on any of the maps. From that point on, the canyon stays narrow, its opposite wall close to the creek. The side the trail passes on is anywhere from 20 or so feet wide, down to just a few feet, the width of the rocks at the edge of the creek, perhaps, and with a rock wall close by on the right.

In June, much of the trail was overhung with low brush, sometimes to the point where it hid the actual tread. But this brush also is the wildflowers, a wide array for such a short hike. The most prevalent is thimbleberry, with ferns tucked at its feet. There also was blooming Clarkia, bunch berry, wild ginger, horsetail, meadow rue, snowberry, fritillaria, camas, penstemon, and several others not identified. There were a few birds, but most of the wildlife was noticed only by sound—the unfortunate crunching that comes when you step on a snail.

Note: The Forest Service hopes to reconstruct this trail in the future, possibly to its full 8.3-mile length.

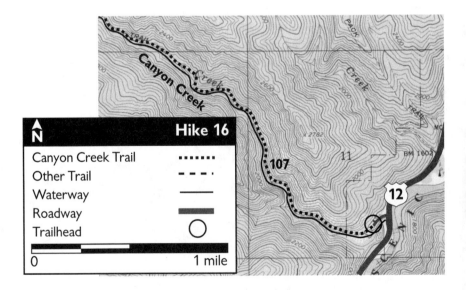

There are several "feline" plants in the Bitterroot and Clearwater Mountains. My favorite is the elegant cat's ears (*Calochortus elegans*). It is also known as the star tulip and is closely related to a couple of other gorgeous, taller, larger-flowered members of the same genus. All are members of the lily family.

The cat's ears are short, usually hiding down in the grass when they bloom in May or June. The flowers are 1 inch across, and have three white petals with purple crescents inside at the base of each. The insides of the flowers are hairy or fuzzy looking.

The flowers of pussy toes (*Antennaria rosea* and others) sit atop a stem and above a rosette of leaves at the base, looking a bit like the more familiar pearly everlasting. The flower is actually a group of tiny composite flowers, each surrounded by pink to rose-colored bracts or modified leaves. They bloom from May to August.

Mountain kittentails (*Synthyris missurica*) have a gorgeous, deep blue-violet flower in the form of a raceme that stands anywhere from 4 to 14 inches above the basal leaves. The leaves are round, toothed on the edges, shiny, evergreen, and have long stems when fully grown. Kittentails bloom at about the same time as the white trillium and yellow glacier lily, and the three make for a smashing combination.

Why: Easy, short hike through cedars 6-foot-plus in diameter.

Ease: Easy, with a 300-plus-foot elevation loss and 400-foot gain over almost 2 miles.

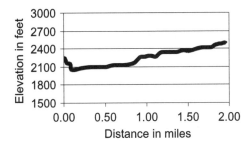

Season: April through November.

Maps: NPNF Visitor Map; USGS Goddard Point, Idaho. (On the Visitor Map, the trail is shown on the wrong side of the creek.)

Information: Fenn Ranger Station, NPNF, 208-926-4258.

Trailhead: Turn on to the road up the Selway River at milepost 97 on Highway 12, then turn right 6.7 miles later to cross the bridge over the Selway. The trailhead is on the left, 3.7 miles up this road.

The Hike: O'Hara Creek can provide a number of different types of short hikes. It can be a 1-mile trip through a forest of cedar, some of them large, with the possibility of a stream-side picnic. It can be a leg-stretcher of anything from 1/2 to 2 miles, given that there will be a couple of stream crossings along the way. And it's just a relatively flat hike, closer to Highway 12 by far than either the trail along the Selway River or that along Meadow Creek.

I've hiked this trail three times and found it to be a pleasant outing, especially the first mile or so. But it can be narrow in places, or covered with overgrown vegetation chest high or more. Early in the season, the creek crossings can be challenging for those not able to walk across flattened logs. Later in the year, at low water, there are several wading options.

The trail is easy to follow, with only a few much narrower and steeper game trails heading off it. It starts with a gentle downhill that takes it to creek level within a half mile—and to one of the best spots along the trail. There is a huge downed tree lying to the left of the trail, moss-covered and with a short tree growing from near its base. Behind it, the stream separates to surround and define a small island.

The first stream crossing is a few yards later. A half-mile walk at creek level and the second stream crossing follow. Then the trail basically heads up and above the creek through a more open area for another mile before it rejoins O'Hara Creek at another fine island, which is a good place for pictures. It's also a natural turnaround spot, for the trail deteriorates after this point.

To get to the second island, take the right fork when the trail splits just after crossing Saddle Creek. The island is a few yards beyond the split. There are two old, burned-out, rugged, and almost hollow snags on the island. It's

Thimbleberry (*Rubus parviflorus*) is a member of the rose family, and its white $1^1/_2$ inch, five-petaled flowers certainly look like roses. But the fruit looks more like a raspberry. Each berry is a multiple fruit, which means that each section of the berry develops from an ovary. All the parts adhere loosely together to form the whole fruit that, when ripe, easily separates from the cone-shaped white receptacle that holds it.

Thimbleberries taste a bit like cranberries and would make lovely jelly, but they do not seem to stay long in prime condition when ripe. They are used by a variety of Native American tribes, either fresh along with other berries, or dried. They also are eaten by both mule and white-tailed deer, and by both black and grizzly bears.

Native Americans used to eat peeled, young shoots, and they used the leaves to line baskets, separate different items in a basket, or as a surface for drying.

Thimbleberry can be anywhere from 2 to 6 feet tall, has large, maplelike leaves up to 6 inches long, and is found throughout Northern Idaho forests. The flowers bloom between May and July and stand in terminal clusters above the leaves. It is a common trailside plant, and its leaves make acceptable biodegradable toilet paper.

hard to imagine that either could withstand a stiff breeze. Each has numerous holes in it, which make interesting spots to look through to view the sky. I wonder if they're the remains of woodpecker activity from long before the trees burned.

I've seen mostly birds along this trail, plus a couple of white-tailed deer. And once, there were more spiders than I care to think about counting. That can happen if you're the first to walk along a trail in the morning.

Connections: This trail theoretically continues along O'Hara Creek and connects to trail FS#338. Neither trail, however, is actively maintained. Check ahead with the Forest Service before planning to hike these connections.

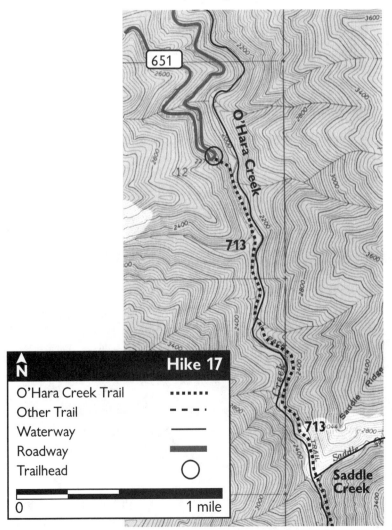

Hike 17

N

O'Hara Creek Trail	·······
Other Trail	– – – ·
Waterway	——
Roadway	▬▬
Trailhead	○

0   1 mile

Why: Spectacular views of Meadow Creek and the Selway-Bitterroot Wilderness, including the entire Gedney Creek basin, the high area above the Three Links Creek basin, Chimney Peak, and the Selway Crags.

Ease: Strenuous, with a 3,800-foot elevation gain over the first 5 miles of trail.

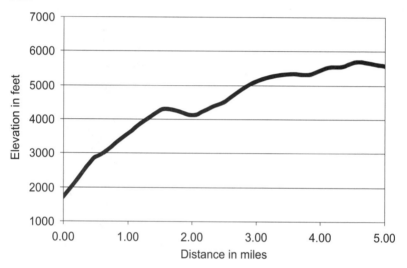

Season: April through November at the trailhead, with a shorter season higher up.

Maps: NPNF Visitor Map; USGS Selway Falls, Idaho, for the first part of the trail, more miles than most need for a day hike. Chimney Peak, Idaho, and Coolwater Mountain, Idaho, have the rest of the trail.

Information: Fenn Ranger Station, NPNF, 208-926-4258.

Trailhead: Turn on to the road along the Selway River at milepost 97 on Highway 12 and drive about 16 miles to Glover Campground and Creek. The trailhead is on the left, just past the creek.

The Hike:

The last time I hiked up Glover Ridge and sat on the hilltop with all the views, a storm with distant and worrisome thunder slowly moved my way. By the time it reached me, the thunder had stopped, and the flat, bottom layer of the clouds was just a few feet above my head. Gray tendrils moved tentatively down from it, as if testing whether it was safe for the cloud to drop down a few more feet to envelop me. Looking to the south, up Meadow Creek, I could see that although the heavy gray clouds hid the hilltops, the creek itself was bathed in sunlight.

The best, and only, apt description for the first 5 miles of this trail is "up." What's amazing is how much "up" there is, for the trail is extremely well-graded. On the way back to the trailhead, I was surprised to discover just how much elevation gain there had been.

The walking is easiest for the first two miles, because there has been more trail use and there is less tall brush overhanging the trail. After a quick view up the Selway, usually topped by a bit of fog early in the morning, the trail covers ground with a series of long, long switchbacks through woods of ponderosa pine and Douglas fir, interrupted about two miles in by a pass through an open brush field. After another couple of miles, the trail turns left at a log held in place by stakes. By then, the brush in the fields has become noticeably shorter and the trees more scarce.

At about mile 5, take another left turn, near what looks like an old road taking off to the right. From then on the trail is out in the open essentially all the time, with occasional snags or trees for relief. As it continues uphill, it passes around the left side of a hill and begins to approach a second hill. The trail will guide left and head around to the left of that hill, too. But before following it there, as you approach the saddle between the two hills, walk off the trail and up the hill on your right. That's the spot for the views, and they are worth every foot of elevation gain. Take an NPNF map along to help with identifying all there is to see.

Glover Ridge was named after Henry Clay Glover, a packer who vacationed in this area between 1918 and 1924.

Connections: For those with good legs and a long hiking range, this trail connects with FS#703 up Boyd Ridge to form the East Boyd Glover Roundtop National Recreation Trail, a total distance of 28 miles of trail and 12 miles of road with an elevation change of more than 5,000 feet. It travels via Roundtop Mountain, which marks the end of the Coolwater Ridge and offers 360-degree views. It is a hard place to get to without a full-sized, four-wheel drive vehicle. If you have one of those, stop at the Fenn Ranger station and ask about driving up. Once on top, this trail can be hiked down from Roundtop, which I did once for a couple of miles.

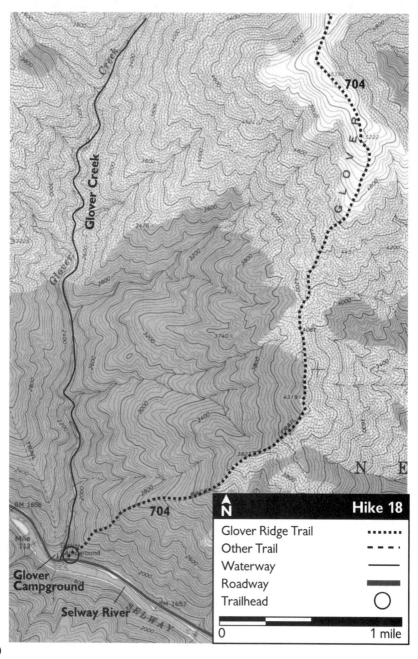

Hike 18	
Glover Ridge Trail	••••••••
Other Trail	– – – ·
Waterway	———
Roadway	▬▬▬
Trailhead	◯
0	1 mile

Why: A level trail along a creek that has carved a beautiful, narrow canyon, plus large Pacific yew trees.

Ease: Easy, with a 200-foot elevation gain over the first 3 miles.

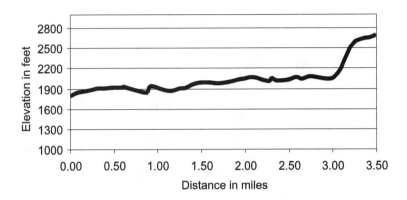

Season: April through November.

Maps: NPNF Visitor Map; USGS Selway Falls, Idaho, and Anderson Butte, Idaho.

Information: Fenn Ranger Station, NPNF, 208-926-4258.

Trailhead: Turn on to the Selway River Road at milepost 97 on Highway 12 and continue about 18 miles to the bridge over the Selway River. Turn right to cross the bridge, then continue along the road for about 1 1/2 miles until it crosses Meadow Creek. Turn right into the parking lot that is just after the bridge, and continue up the gravel drive to the trailhead and pit toilet. Note the large Pacific yew between the parking places and the creek at the camping area.

The Hike: There is no shortage of reasons to hike the trail along Meadow Creek. The canyon is gorgeous, narrow and deep, and lined with cedar that provide shade most all the way. The understory is varied but always green. The largest Pacific yew I've ever seen live along this trail and in the parking lot, some with trunks more than a foot in diameter. There have been times when they've been decorated with the red berries that the yew have in place of cones. Rock outcrops dot both sides of the canyon, some eroded into caves and cubbyholes and some featuring mosses and lichens. The creek itself is wide and slow in stretches, and sometimes, when the canyon's rock walls hem it in, narrow and fast, as if it's rushing to get to those slow and quieter places.

I've always seen interesting birds along this trail, whether a large flock of ruffed grouse, a dipper, or a belted kingfisher. I also have been face to face with a small bat, hovering a foot away from my nose as we inspected each other.

The area is special enough that it has been proposed for wilderness more than once. It was part of the Selway-Bitterroot Primitive Area that predated wilderness designation, but it was not included in the wilderness.

There are no side trails or detours in the first 3 miles of trail. At Rabbit Creek, about 2 miles in, there is a good campsite, as there is at Little Creek. Because little sun reaches the canyon floor, however, they both are rather cool spots for early season camping.

The trail is closed to motorized vehicles after these first 3 miles.

Connections: The trail continues for a total of 15 miles to Meadow Creek Cabin, which can be rented, and is the point of departure for hikes in four directions. Check with the Forest Service before planning to hike that far.

Pacific yew (*Taxus brevifolia*), also known as the Western yew, is a large shrub or small tree (up to 20 or 30 feet tall) that grows in the shade or understory of the forest. Its needles look much like those of a fir or spruce or hemlock, but they are dark green above, lighter below, $1/2$ to 1 inch long, and lay flat in two rows. They have sharp tips.

Yew have a "messy" growth habit when compared to small fir, spruce, or hemlock. But the best identifiers are the berries, when there, and the bark. The berries are like those of domestic yew—red, fleshy, and open ended. They are also poisonous. The bark is thin and peels, the old purplish bark on the outside giving way to the newer, reddish inner bark.

The tree is slow growing and produces no seed cones, just the red berries. Its trunk is twisted and fluted, usually 1 foot or less in diameter, though most are much smaller. The wood is hard and polishes well, is liked by woodcarvers, and is famous for being made into archery bows. Its bark was the original source of taxol, found to be effective against certain cancers, especially ovarian and breast.

It is a preferred winter browse for moose.

Why: Level trail along a lovely river, with fast and easy access to the Selway-Bitterroot Wilderness.

Ease: Easy, with a 200-foot net elevation gain over the first 5 to 6 miles of trail.

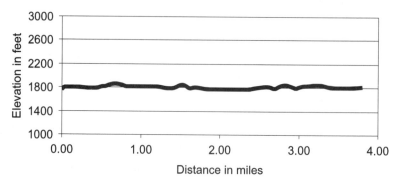

Season: April through November.

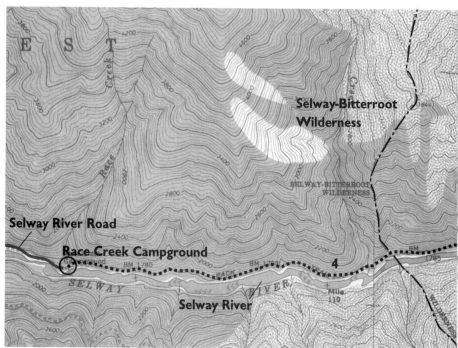

Maps: NPNF Visitor Map; USGS Selway Falls, Idaho, and Fog Mountain, Idaho.

Information: Fenn Ranger Station, NPNF, 208-926-4258.

Trailhead: Turn on to the Selway River Road at milepost 97 on Highway 12 and continue about 19 miles until the road ends at Race Creek campground. The trailhead is in the lower parking lot.

The Hike:

> The Selway River is known for its rattlesnakes. One of the first I saw there was the largest rattler I ever hope to see. In my memory, it was as thick as my forearm. That snake dropped off the trail as I neared, as most do. Then it appeared to have second thoughts about the danger I posed and headed back up toward the trail. I moved on without delay.
>
> Another rattler along this trail apparently uses the ostrich approach when humans come near, hiding its head and leaving the rest of its body on the trail. Both of these snakes illustrate what may be too obvious to mention: The Selway's rattlers aren't much afraid of what they see of us humans. Beware.

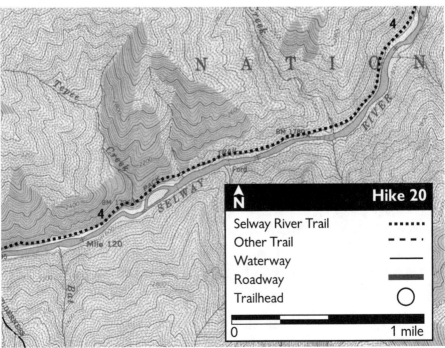

Hike 20

Selway River Trail	•••••••
Other Trail	– – – '
Waterway	——
Roadway	▬▬▬
Trailhead	○

0   1 mile

There also are garter snakes and rubber boas along this trail. Rubber boas (*Charina bottae*) are personal favorites. They're monochromatic, usually taupe colored, blunt at both ends, and always slow moving. They, like other boas, constrict their prey— usually young mice and shrews for the rubber boas. I've had a couple of them try to warm up by getting next to me when I sat down to take a break.

The downhill out of the parking lot may be the stiffest grade this trail has to offer, at least for the first 6 miles to Cupboard Creek. Once down that tiny hill, the biggest problem is finding shade in the middle of the day. Although there are trees along and above the trail, they are sparse. Hiking early or late on a hot day makes a great deal of sense.

The canyon is steep but does not feel close because the river is wide through these first miles. It is always possible to hear the river from the trail, almost always possible to see it. During the floating season, there may be kayakers or rafters along the river, adding somewhat out-of-place bright colors to the greens, grays, and blues of the canyon.

The wilderness boundary is $1\frac{1}{2}$ miles from the trailhead. The trail regularly crosses creeks, so even though the trail is usually several feet above the river, there is water available to filter or purify.

There are many good spots to stop along the trail, either to camp or just to take a break. Some have beaches and calm water, though during high water many would be much less than the 200 feet from water requirement for camping in the wilderness. Actually, during high water, some would be under water.

It is a well-used trail, hiked more than most if the number of different boot prints is any indication, and though it's certainly used by stock, there's not as much evidence of that as one would expect.

There are no side trails along the 6 miles except those down to fishing holes or campsites, and the trail is closed to motorized vehicles from the trailhead.

The Selway River was named for Thomas Selway, a sheep rancher from Beaverhead County, Montana, who ran large flocks in the Selway area from the 1890s through the early 1900s.

Connections: This trail continues for a total of 28 miles to the Moose Creek Ranger Station and 50 miles to the Paradise Guard Station.

Why: History along a short trail to a campsite Lewis and Clark used on their 1806 return journey east.

Ease: Easy $1/3$ mile in length with an approximate 280-foot elevation change.

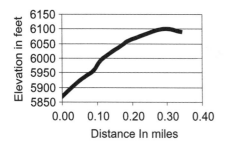

Season: Mid-July through late September.

Maps: CWNF Visitor Map; USGS Rocky Point, Idaho. (The campsite is noted on both maps, but the trail is not.)

Information: Powell Ranger District, CWNF, 208-942-3113.

Trailhead: On the left at Powell Junction, mile 5.7 from Highway 12 on the Parachute Hill Road heading up to the Motorway.

The Hike: Lewis and Clark reached the campsite in the saddle at the top of this small hill on the evening of June 28, 1806. On the advice of their Nez Perce guides, they stopped early so their horses could feed on the grassy southern slopes of the hill.

The trail segment to the campsite is part of both the ancient Lolo Trail across the Bitterroot Mountains and the historic Nez Perce Trail followed by Lewis and Clark as they traveled east on the morning after they camped on the hillside. It is not part of any trail system developed by the Forest Service, and is distinct from the Bird-Truax Trail that was constructed where the road is now, along the northern side of this hill.

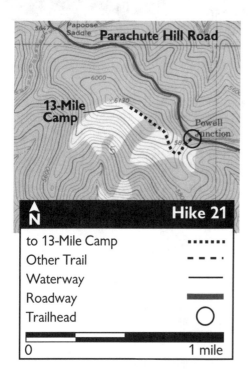

The hiking trail begins at the left of the historic signpost. It heads gently, then more steeply uphill through evergreens with a huckleberry and beargrass understory. In the open meadow about $1/2$ mile in, the trail becomes indistinct, even non-existent. Before turning right at that point and heading up the hill to the campsite, you might want to tie a bandanna to a tree near the spot where the trail leaves the woods, for this place won't be obvious when you head back down to find it. Or use the natural and man-made landmarks already in place by carefully noting your position with respect to the bench or flat open area below on the left, as well as the roads in the distance to the left.

Although there is no distinct trail through the open meadow and up the hill to the campsite, the site is easy to find. Just head uphill. Near the top, there is a sparse wooded area. Walk through it and on to the top, then down a bit to the saddle before the next high point. This saddle contains the campsite area now known as 13-Mile Camp, so named because it is 13 miles from Lewis and Clark's previous camp at Spring Mountain.

Western gold thread (*Coptis occidentalis*) is a common trailside plant. It is the foliage that is most often seen, for the barely noticeable flowers are tiny, $1/4$ to $1/2$ inch wide, white, and early, in April and May. The leaves are evergreen and basal, the latter meaning there are not any growing up the flower stem. They are shiny, leathery, broadly oval in shape, and have serrated edges. They are arranged in groups of three at the end of the stems, and each of the three is shallowly divided into three lobes.

The leaves look similar to those of the wood anemone (*Anemone piperi*), but the anemone's leaves are more pointed, and it has a much larger five-petaled white flower, is deciduous, and the plant stands 6 to 14 inches tall. Gold thread is just 2 to 5 inches tall.

Gold thread grows in older, shady forests, and its tubular petals produce nectar at the tips. The plant is named for its bright yellow rhizomes, and there is sometimes a bit of yellow at the base of the leaf stalks, too. In the early 1800s, gold thread was sold in Boston drug stores because it was thought to help with mouth ulcerations.

Why: Beautiful lakes in a wet meadow and views of the scenic area above the Silver Creek drainage.

Ease: Moderate, with a 220-foot elevation gain and 820-foot loss in the 2½ miles to the first lake, then a level mile past the second lake and to the saddle beyond the third lake. One section of the trail down to the first lake is rocky, eroded, and steep.

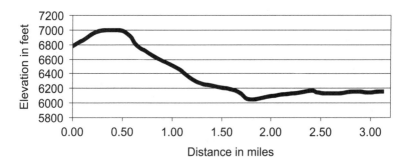

Season: Mid-July through late September.

Maps: CWNF Visitor Map; USGS Cayuse Junction, Idaho.

Information: Powell Ranger District, CWNF, 208-942-3113.

Trailhead: On the right at mile 10.3 on the Motorway.

The Hike: When I hiked down to the Lost Lakes during the fire season of 2000, heavy smoke obscured the views that I knew must be there but couldn't be seen. The next year, I saw them: views of the Bitterroot divide to the north, southeast, and east, and of Williams and Rhodes Peaks to the north. The jagged, black ridge that connects Kelly's Finger with Blacklead Mountain framed the view on the west, and the tip of Kelly's Finger was in the background.

Even without views, the Lost Lakes are well worth the hike. They sit in a flat, marshy meadow framed by evergreen hills, perfect lunch spots for a late summer day.

The trail heads uphill for a half mile out of the small parking area before topping out and heading along the ridgeline that separates the Fox and Cayuse Creek drainages. Along the ridge, it is possible to see the Rocky Point lookout and beyond, over the checkerboard lands of Idaho to the high Bitterroot Divide that separates Idaho and Montana.

The downhill off the ridge starts gently, with a rocky outcropped hillside on the left and a meadow below on the right. The latter is dotted with trees, rocks, and low grouse whortleberry and grass. Then the trail gets ratty—steep, rocky, rooty, and washed out. It must resemble a sluice box when water is running in the spring. But if the sky is clear, it's along this stretch

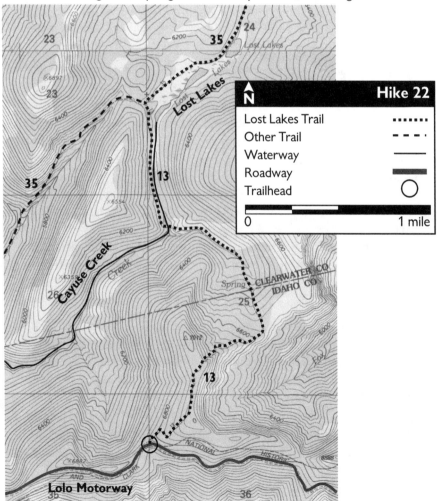

	Hike 22
Lost Lakes Trail	....
Other Trail	- - - ·
Waterway	———
Roadway	▬▬▬
Trailhead	○
0	1 mile

that the high areas above the Silver Creek drainage can be seen, making it hard to do what's necessary, which is to watch where to place your feet on the trail.

After a mile or so of downhill, the trail heads back into the trees, through an area that is all green except for tree trunks and a few rock outcrops. In wet areas, there is a mass of royal blue gentian in season, especially along the small, intermittent, and unnamed creek the trail crosses and then parallels until it reaches Cayuse Creek, 2½ miles into the hike.

The creek bed opens up at that junction, and Cayuse Creek meanders through a flat, grassy, marshy area that continues, then expands to surround the Lost Lakes that sit in the headwaters of the Cayuse. In the early fall, the meadow is golden-brown. In early summer, it is an equally pleasing bright green. The first lake comes into view within a few hundred yards and is just a widening of the creek.

Shortly thereafter, the trail junctions with the one from Cayuse Junction (hike 23), and the two continue on, hugging the edge of the marshy meadow until they reach the second lake after a few hundred yards. There are well-used campsites here, off the trail on the nonlake side. The meadow also has a few gentian, low bushes, and a scattering of small trees, and it is surrounded by woods that sit on higher ground. While there are ample bugs early in the season, by late August it's as good a lunch spot as you can find anywhere.

Connections: This trail connects with the one to Cayuse Junction (hike 23), which connects with the trail up Silver Creek to Goat Lake, FS#248. Although the latter provides access to Blacklead Mountain and the nearby high country of Clearwater River that is seen from this hike, the trails in that area are classified as way trails and, as such, are not well-maintained and can be difficult to follow. Trail FS#248 is a secondary trail, occasionally maintained.

The checkerboard lands result from the federal government's attempt to encourage the railroads to move west. The government gave square miles of publicly owned land to the railroads, which alternated with square miles retained in public ownership. The land that remained publicly owned is currently part of the national forest system, and on forest maps, the two ownerships are shown in different colors. Hence, the term "checkerboard." The lands given to the railroads are owned primarily by timber companies now.

Why: Fine meadows and lakes.

Ease: Moderate, with a 1,040-foot elevation gain in the 3.5 miles to the lakes, another mile of almost-level hiking to the saddle past the third lake.

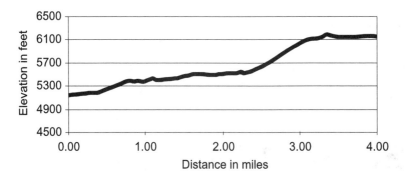

Season: Mid-July through late September.

Maps: CWNF Visitor Map; USGS Cayuse Junction, Idaho, shows the trail to the lakes. USGS Rhodes Peak, Idaho, shows the trail beyond them but is not necessary for this hike.

Information: Powell Ranger District, CWNF, 208-942-3113.

Trailhead: On the right, at the horseshoe bend 1.3 miles along the Toboggan Ridge Road (#581). Toboggan Ridge Road is on the right at mile 17.9 on the Motorway.

The Hike: I am of two minds about this trail. The Lost Lakes are definitely worth hiking to, especially late in the season when the bugs are fewer. Cayuse Creek is lovely, clear and clean. Its headwaters are at the Lost Lakes. But there are two ways to get to the lakes, this hike and the previous hike. This one is slightly easier, for the 1,040 feet in elevation gain to the lakes is spread over $3\frac{1}{2}$ miles rather than split into 820 feet in loss and 220 in gain over $2\frac{1}{2}$ miles heading in via hike 22.

But hike 22 gives you spectacular views, whereas this trail offers none. And although this trail parallels Cayuse Creek for most of the way to the lakes, it spends little time near the creek or even with the creek in view. It also has a $^3/_4$ mile section of trail near the end that goes up 600 steep feet.

Be that as it may, this trail sticks to the woods, staying in the narrow Cayuse Creek canyon until it hits the Lost Lakes. It crosses Silver Creek about $^1/_4$ mile in, and the trail up Silver Creek takes off to the left after another $^1/_4$ mile. Crossing Silver Creek is not difficult, but downed trees hid the trail in 2001. If they are still there, stay to the right while crossing.

The steep uphill occurs after Cayuse Creek splits off to the right, to flow around two small peaks before reaching the Lost Lakes. The trail follows an unnamed creek branch, and the steep section ends as the trail crosses the headwaters of that branch. This is a lovely spot of bright green sedges and other plants, as well as blooming heather and shooting stars. Shortly thereafter, the trail crosses a saddle, another pleasant spot of low vegetation and small trees, and heads down to junction with FS#13, which is the trail down to the lakes from the Motorway (hike 22).

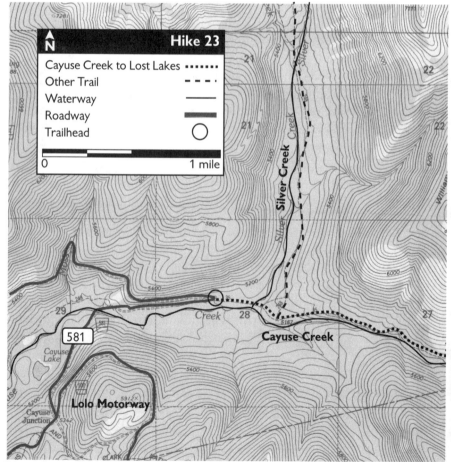

Heading left, the second of the lakes comes into view in $1/4$ mile. The trail then goes into woods again before it passes the third lake. (The first Lost Lake is seen on the way out, through the trees.) Beyond the third lake, it crosses a small saddle that separates the Cayuse Creek headwaters from those of a creek that eventually drains into the Crooked Fork.

There are mile markers on trees along the trail that note mile 1 and mile 2. I'm not sure about their accuracy. The space between the two seems to be a mile, but the distance between the 1-mile marker and the trailhead took 40 minutes to hike. I believe that for whatever reason, the 1-mile marker must denote the distance from the junction of this trail with the one up Silver Creek. Then the elapsed hiking time makes sense.

Connections: This trail connects with the one down to the lakes from the Motorway (hike 22), and to the trail up Silver Creek, FS#248.

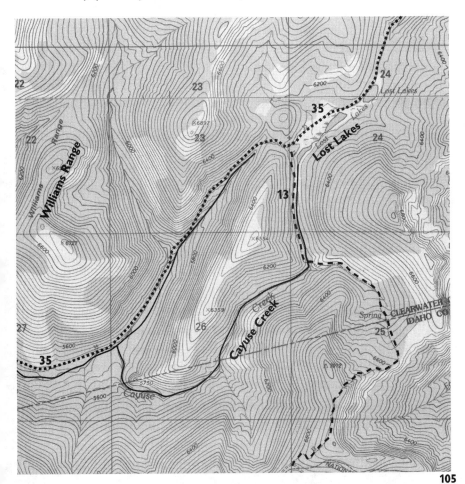

Why: A gentle up-and-down hike with superb views, pink rocks, and if the timing is right, fields of flowers.

Ease: Easy, ½ mile over a hill.

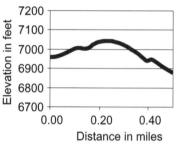

Season: Mid-July through late September.

Maps: CWNF Visitor Map; USGS Indian Post Office, Idaho. (The latter shows more trail on the ground than is hikeable.)

Information: Powell Ranger District, CWNF, 208-942-3113.

Trailheads: On the left, at miles 26.3 and 26.7 on the Motorway.

The Hike: The old Nez Perce Trail followed by Lewis and Clark dropped off the ridge at Indian Post Office and headed north and west into the Moon Creek drainage. On the evening of September 16, 1805, after a long and difficult day of keeping to the trail despite heavy snowfall, Clark and an advance party reached Moon Creek and stopped to build an encampment. Lewis and the rest of the Corps caught up later and were greeted by warm fires. Joseph Whitehouse called this place a "lonesome cove" in his journal, and that name was adopted years later when the Forest Service named the various Lewis and Clark camping spots.

By 1866, the Nez Perce had started to use an alternate route for travel in this area. It stayed on the main ridge between Moon Saddle and Indian Post Office. Explorers after that time mentioned Indian Post Office Lakes, visible from that ridge trail, while the Corps of Discovery did not.

The Bird-Truax Trail in this area followed neither route but kept to a wagon-road grade on the north side of the ridge. Essentially all of these historic trails are obscured by brush and downfall today.

Indian Post Office first appeared on maps with the place name "Indian Monuments," a name that probably referred to the rock cairns of unknown origin that sit on the ridge. In later years, rumors spread suggesting that the rocks were used to hold messages. It is unlikely that this actually occurred, and none of the early explorers mentioned monuments or rock cairns in their journals. Steve notes that none of the rock cairns in place today were there in 1988.

From the easternmost trailhead, the trail heads uphill through sparse beargrass and mountain heather. Along it there are many chances for wide, sweeping views south of the Bitterroot Divide and the country between it and the Motorway. The contrast is of interest, between the wild, relatively untouched areas and the clear cuts in many sizes and shapes.

The trail is more or less distinct as it heads to the left of the rocky area on top of the hill, where the pink rocks are. Beyond the rocks, on the other side of the hill, the trail is faint, if visible at all. Just head down the point of the ridgeline, past a series of rock cairns. The views from this side also are worth time and include the only area I've seen in the Clearwater National Forest that's above tree line except for Pot Mountain. (The area is seen much more closely from hike 22.) It is near the Montana border, north of Lolo Pass. Rhodes Peak is the highest point, long and light colored from this vantage point and looking like it is made of different rocks than anything around it. Williams Peak is to the southwest of Rhodes, bumpy and dark, and the ridge from Blacklead Mountain to Kelly's Finger also is bumpy and dark. Up close, this is a spectacularly beautiful area, especially in the fall when the huckleberry have turned color.

Note: Historic cairns often commemorate a loved one or a special event. They also were, and are, used as trail markers. They are not built to contain items within them.

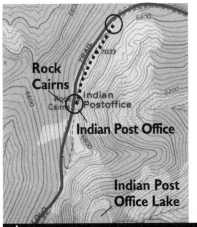

Rock Cairns

Indian Postoffice

Indian Post Office

Indian Post Office Lake

Hike 24

Indian Post Office	·······
Other Trail	— — ·
Waterway	——
Roadway	▬▬
Trailhead	○

0   1 mile

The Sinque Hole, Indian Grave, and Smoking Place FS#25/40

Why: History, pleasant woods, interesting rocks, a few views, and the water hole surrounded by a small, bright green meadow that is reported in the Lewis and Clark journals.

Ease: Easy, 2-plus-mile trail with an 800-foot elevation gain from the eastern trailhead to the Smoking Place, then a 200-foot drop to the western trailhead. Half-mile segments separate the historic sites along the way (see note at the end of this hike).

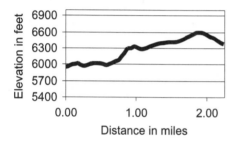

Season: Mid-July through late September.

Maps: CWNF Visitor Map; USGS Holly Creek, Idaho, and Lookout Peak, Idaho. (The 1984 photorevised editions of these USGS maps do not show the trail.)

Information: Lochsa Ranger District, CWNF, 208-926-4274.

Trailheads: There are two trailheads, one on either side of 12-Mile Saddle, at miles 37.2 and 40.4 on the Motorway. Each is marked with a post that indicates it is a historical trail, and signs with mileage information are a few yards up the trail at each end. (Note: There is little parking at the east trailhead. Park either in the turnout about 1/8 mile east of the trailhead, or use the parking area near the west trailhead and hike in the reverse direction.)

The Hike:

> It would be difficult, if not impossible, to find a trail more intertwined with history and more demanding of respect and contemplation. There's a Lewis and Clark campsite, a Nez Perce

sacred site, the grave site of a young Native American, a traditional hunting camp, and a fire lookout site.

On September 17, 1805, the Lewis and Clark party climbed wearily out of the Gravey Creek drainage and back on to the main ridge. Along the way they passed the Sinque Hole, so named because it resembled a feature that occurs in Kentucky, Virginia, and similar areas. Sinque holes occur when water percolates through limestone and creates a cavern in the rock. If the top of the cavern caves in, there is a hole. If the bottom outlet becomes plugged, the hole fills with water and looks much like what is seen here.

Expedition member Private Joseph Whitehouse noted in his journal that they "camped at a small branch on a mountain; near a round deep Sinque hole which was full of water." It had been a cold, wet, snow-filled day, and the southern exposure and open campsite area were appealing. Steve's research suggests that they camped at what's now known as Indian Grave Camp, although the CWNF maps note that they camped at the Sinque Hole. Whitehouse also mentioned that wolves howled during much of that night, and they saw some sign of deer and were optimistic about finding game ahead. Unfortunately, this was not to be. The next day, Clark and six hunters went ahead of the main party to hunt game and scout the trail. The two groups remained separated until they met several days later on the Weippe Prairie.

The campsite at Indian Grave is at the head of Indian Grave Creek, where it leaves the wet meadow above the trail. The area was named "Swampy Saddle" by the Bird-Truax Expedition, an appropriate name since most anytime you visit the meadow, it is wet and swampy. In 1866, the Bird-Truax Expedition built this trail, and the Forest Service made use of it from the time it began managing the area in 1907 until the Motorway was completed in the fall of 1934.

The fire lookout at Indian Grave Peak was located on the top of the peak. Because it was considered critical for the region, the Forest Service constructed a road from Musselshell Meadows to the peak. The construction plans for this road, which is the western end of the Lolo Motorway, were described in a report in November 1929. The road was completed about 1934, its construction combined with that of the Motorway. The lookout was dismantled and moved to Horseshoe Lake sometime after 1963, and the road was closed in order to protect the meadow and grave at Swampy Saddle.

> Swampy Saddle was a popular hunters' camp until the access road to the lookout was closed, and some hunters continue to use the area today. Steve's grandfather had the outfitter permit for the area in the early 1930s. He sometimes used Indian Grave Camp as a spike camp, a temporary camp set up about a half-day's ride from the base camp and moved as needed during the hunting season. Steve's family photo album has an old, blurred black-and-white photo of his great-great aunt Nora cooking there.

The name "Indian Grave" honors a teenaged Nez Perce boy who died there about 1895. The Mallickan family was traveling the Lolo Trail and stopped late in the day to camp at Swampy Saddle. They prepared a hasty meal. The next day the entire family became ill, and Albert Parsons Mallickan died. Although it is not possible to know for certain what made everyone sick, it is generally thought that it was food poisoning, and that Albert, an active teenager of about 14, probably ate more than anyone else. The family marked the current gravesite about 1960, and family members still visit it.

The Smoking Place was visited by Lewis and Clark on their return trip across the mountains in 1806. They stopped at midday on June 27 and smoked with their Nez Perce guides at a rock cairn that Clark described as a conic mound of stones six or eight feet high, with a pine pole about 15 feet long. Clark was reflective in his journal that day, writing, "after having smoked the pipe and contemplating this scene sufficient to have damped the spirits of any except such hardy travelers as we have become, we continued our march." He was reflecting on the jumbled mess of the Bitterroot Mountains that they still had to cross before they returned to the plains and the rivers in the East.

The rock cairn is no longer there, but new and smaller ones have been erected in its place.

From the east trailhead, the trail to the Sinque Hole is level to gently uphill through lodgepole pine woods. When it nears the Sinque Hole, the trail begins to head slightly downhill into the saddle between the next ridge and the one it has been below and along. There is a small rock outcrop atop a flat area to the right, and a larger rocky area in front, on the other side of the trail. To the left of this second rocky area, there is a hole in the tree canopy. That hole exactly pinpoints the Sinque Hole. To see it, leave the trail

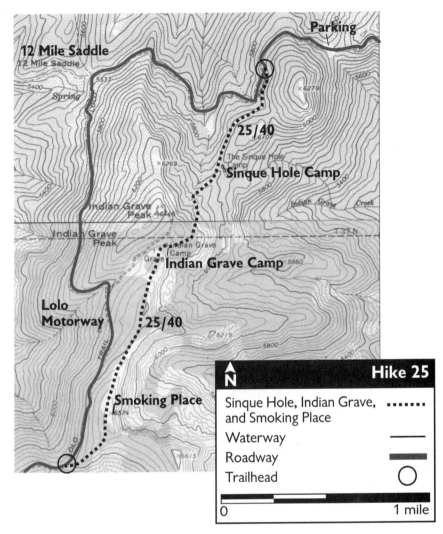

Hike 25

Sinque Hole, Indian Grave, and Smoking Place	·······
Waterway	——
Roadway	▭
Trailhead	○

0   1 mile

and head toward the larger rocky area. (Note: The bright green meadow area around the water hole is fragile. Please do not walk on it.)

From the Sinque Hole, the trail heads gently uphill through a rocky area, then more steeply along the Indian Grave Peak hillside on the right. Near the top of this section of trail, there are views of Grave Peak to the south east and across the Lochsa River. It is the highest mountain between the Motorway and that section of the Bitterroot Mountains. Its peak is treed on the upriver side, open on the downriver side, and has a flat area extending downriver that terminates in a small, conical tip. In the other direction, it is possible to see the Moose Creek Buttes, which lie at the junction of Kelly Creek and the North Fork of the Clearwater River. They are a bit flat topped too, but pinkish tan in color and without visible trees or peaks.

Once over the top of the climb, the trail heads generally downhill, then left at the fork just before crossing a creek via a rock and dirt bridge. The bright green, boggy meadow that is visible above the creek is known as "Indian Grave Camp" and has been used over the years both by hunters and by the Nez Perce.

The gravesite is to the right of the trail after the creek crossing. It is surrounded by a pole barricade that encloses the gravestone of Albert Parsons Mallickan. From the grave, the trail continues by way of a series of ups and downs past several interesting piles of rock, some of which look like they couldn't possibly have been placed by nature.

The sign for the Smoking Place is on the left or upper side of the trail about $3/4$ mile from the Mallickan grave. The Smoking Place is up the hill, above the sign, on an open and flattened ridgetop. It is a sacred site for the Nez Perce Indians and should be treated with respect.

In addition to being a place to sit quietly and think, the Smoking Place also offers fine views in almost all directions. Unfortunately, some of them show too many of the straight lines characteristic of human activity on the land.

It is another $1/3$ mile of downhill walking to the west trailhead through woods similar to those already walked: lodgepole pine, Douglas fir, subalpine fir, and a low understory that is primarily herbaceous. Unless you arranged for a car to be parked there or you want a little more exercise, I suggest turning around after visiting the Smoking Place and heading back to the east trailhead.

Note: Although the signs at both trailheads say that all of the above places are $1/2$ mile apart, that's not the case. It's about $1/2$ mile from the east trailhead to the Sinque Hole, a bit more than that from there to the Indian Grave, $3/4$ mile from the Indian Grave to the Smoking Place, and about $1/3$ mile from there to the west trailhead.

Why: This is a trail that would be hiked more often if it was easier to get to. The woods are nice, and in the fall, there is great color. There are occasional excellent views in several directions, and there is history, for the trail follows a route that has been traveled for hundreds of years.

Ease: Moderate, with a 700-foot elevation gain over the first 5 to 6 miles.

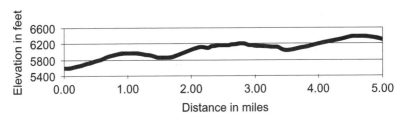

Season: Mid-July through late September.

Maps: CWNF Visitor Map; USGS Lookout Peak, Idaho.

Information: North Fork Ranger District, CWNF, 208-476-4541.

Trailhead: The trailhead is located on the right at 12-mile Saddle, mile 38.3 on the Motorway. It is at the back of the parking lot and camping area, where there is a trailhead sign that reads, "Trail 167/164, Bear Butte Trail."

The Hike: The Windy Ridge Trail route has been used for hundreds of years for travel between the North Fork of the Clearwater River and the Lochsa and Selway River areas. The original trail was rerouted somewhat after 1907, however, when the Forest Service began to use it as a link between the North Fork and the Lolo Trail.

The camp at 12-mile Saddle became firmly established after the Lolo Motorway was completed in 1935. It is a popular hunting camp and in the fall is completely filled with vehicles and hunters heading for the North Fork area. The Windy Ridge Camp noted on the maps is an old sheep camp dating from when the trail was used to move sheep from the Superior Stock Driveway north of Windy Ridge to the grass at nearby Indian Grave Camp.

The Superior Stock Driveway was used in the first half of the twentieth century to move sheep and cattle between the railroad in Superior, Montana, and the meadows of Pierce, Weippe, and Fraser, Idaho. It followed the Lolo Trail for a short distance before heading northeast, to grazing in the fire-enriched meadows of the North Fork.

Beginning in 1922, sheep grazed Cook Mountain, the Windy Ridge area, and Gravy Creek. By 1930, the driveway was shown on forest maps as the

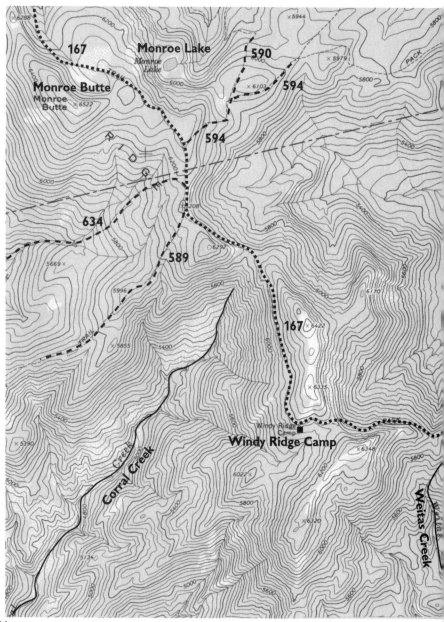

"stock driveway," but by then, the fields opened by the fires of 1910 and 1919 had begun to grow in with brush and trees, making them less valuable for grazing. The last sheep used the driveway in 1948, the last cattle in 1952.

People also traveled the driveway from Superior to the Weippe and Pierce country, possibly joining the returning stockmen for safety and companionship.

The trail heads up from 12-mile Saddle, through woods and then along the north side of a rocky outcrop. The views from here are of an attractive ridge to the west, of Lookout Peak about 5 miles beyond to the north, and of the much less picturesque, heavily roaded and cut Gravy Creek drainage to the northeast.

Once over the saddle that connects the ridge this trail is on with the ridge it is approaching, the trail will head behind the latter on its west side. Occasional views into the upper Corral Creek drainage are available from there, as well as glimpses through the trees of the area of the Motorway to the west: Willow Ridge, Sherman Peak, No-see-um Butte, Bald Mountain, and Castle Butte, all but the last known to have been traveled by Lewis and Clark.

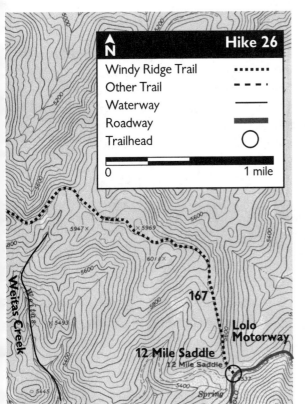

There is a spring below the trail partway along in this section. Although it doesn't offer a view, in hot weather it's a fine place to sit on rocks next to the water and enjoy a cooling break.

At the corner where the trail passes over the top of the Corral Creek drainage, there is a glimpse of the Selway Crags to the southwest, and there is a 19-mile marker sign on one of the trees. Where the tree is 19 miles from is a mystery to me. After crossing the next saddle, the trail again heads uphill, first through an open area, then through more woods, and over a couple more saddles. From the open area it is possible to see a small bit of one of the most beautiful and rugged spots around, though it is many miles away. The jagged ridges to the east are near Rhodes Peak and the Idaho–Montana border, one of the few areas above timberline in this section of Idaho. It is a view from a different angle of the area also seen from the Lost Lakes Trail (hike 22) and from Indian Post Office (hike 24).

There are two trails off to the left near the $4\frac{1}{2}$-mile mark, about $\frac{1}{8}$ mile apart, and they are followed after another $\frac{1}{8}$ mile or so by a trail off to the right, at a sign that says, "5 miles to Motorway and 12-Mile Saddle."

The trail then heads northwest past Monroe Butte on the left and the steep, wooded drop off to Monroe Lake on the right. The lake is visible only in tiny glimpses even if, just as the trail begins to lose altitude as it passes Monroe Butte, you drop off the trail on to a flat area below on the right. But it's not really worth the effort, for only tiny snatches of lake are visible through the tree branches.

Connections: This trail continues for a total of $13\frac{1}{2}$ miles to Cook Mountain. Trail FS#167 continues from there to Bear Butte and then down along Fourth of July Creek to the North Fork of the Clearwater River. Along the way there are old growth hemlock and fantastic views of the North Fork country, especially Pot Mountain.

The three trails that junction with #167 at $4\frac{1}{2}$ to 5 miles in are maintained primarily by hunters, if at all. Trail FS#634 to the left and down Windy Creek is listed as part of the Idaho Centennial Trail but is poorly maintained and difficult traveling. It connects with trail FS#174 along Weitas Creek. Trail FS#174 also can be reached at a second 12-mile Saddle trailhead (appendix), or from the road to Liz Butte (hike 32).

Why: Views, especially of the Selway Crags but also of Bald Mountain and a few of the Seven Devils.

Ease: Moderate, with an approximate 600-foot elevation change over $1^1/_2$ miles of trail.

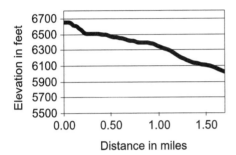

Season: Mid-July through late September.

Maps: CWNF Visitor Map; USGS Holly Creek, Idaho. (The trail is not shown in the right place on the former and is not shown at all on the latter.)

Information: Lochsa Ranger District, CWNF, 208-926-4274.

Trailhead: At the end of the Castle Butte Road, which is a left off the Motorway at mile 44.2. There is a trail sign at the edge of the parking area below the lookout.

The Hike: The trail starts as an old road that heads downhill past a couple of water or oil tanks and past a second sign stating that the trail ends in 2 miles. It soon changes from a road to a trail, after which it switchbacks down under the lookout and provides a superb view of the Selway Crags. It is a different view than the one from farther west on the Motorway and well worth this short trip down. (If you're feeling really lazy, walk up to the base of the lookout instead to see the same thing.)

Once down the hill about 200 feet, the trail heads northwest, loosely following the hill's contour, until it reaches a dirt road and a hunter's camp. Follow the road a few yards to the left to a signpost for the trail. Head to its left, through beargrass, shrubs, and trees on a somewhat indistinct trail. It will lead into the open below the top of the hill and with a rock cairn in view ahead. Walk toward the cairn. Round-topped Sherman Peak soon will appear in the distance, above a saddle with a clearly visible trail through it. That is where to go, passing a second cairn along the way. (The open meadow at the top of the hill, however, is the place for those Bald Mountain views.)

For about 1³/₄ miles, the trail is two tracks through a pleasant woods, an old road most likely. The understory is low throughout, the woods open and comfortable walking. Then the trail becomes steeper and becomes one rather than two tracks. It peters out soon after, just before a pile of rocks. Unless you're out for exercise, there's really no point in going beyond the double track.

Castle Butte was so named because before its top was flattened for the building of the lookout, the rocks were said to resemble a castle. The views from the lookout are quite fine in all directions.

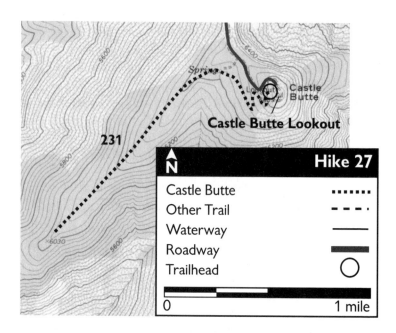

Castle Butte Lookout

N	**Hike 27**
Castle Butte	•••••••
Other Trail	– – – ·
Waterway	——
Roadway	▬▬
Trailhead	○

0   1 mile

Why: A short hike to a quiet lake and great picnic spot.

Ease: Easy, with a 300-foot elevation loss over the 1-mile trail down to the lake.

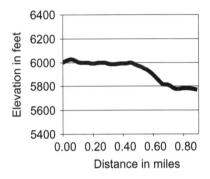

Season: Mid-July through late September.

Maps: CWNF Visitor Map; USGS Holly Creek, Idaho. (The trail is not on the latter.)

Information: North Fork Ranger District, CWNF, 208-476-4541.

Trailhead: The trailhead is on the right at mile 45.3 on the Motorway, on a tight corner that is at the base of a short, rough road used by hunters to reach camping areas above the road.

The Hike:

> When I hiked this trail during the year 2000, there was one place near the bottom, right before the lake, where many of the trees were missing large strips of bark. My first thought was that an enormous troop of hungry porcupines had spent time there. But porcupine damage usually is higher up in the tree, in what's called the "sugar zone," a three to four foot section near the crown leader and a bit below the top. Usually porcupines girdle the tree and kill the crown, damaging the tree and often killing it if the tree is young. Porcupines prefer yellow or ponderosa pines, with lodgepole pine as the second choice.

What I saw that day was black bear damage. Black bears also eat the sugar-rich cambium layer located just under the bark, but they strip the bark closer to the ground than porcupines do and often damage whole groves of trees. Bears usually eat the cambium in spring, when they've come out of hibernation and are quite hungry. It's also the time that the young trees are just starting to grow and take up the sugars that have been stored in their root systems all winter.

The trail starts at the short, rough, old road that goes uphill for a bit. But once at the top of the hill, it starts down, narrows, and comes to look more like a trail than a road. A second trail sign at the top of the hill reads that the lake is 1 mile distant.

The grade down to the lake is reasonable, and the trail stays in the trees, which are primarily lodgepole pine, with fir, spruce, and hemlock interspersed. The understory is standard huckleberry, beargrass and whortleberry.

The lake can be seen off to the left a couple of minutes before the trail's end at a small camping spot near the lake's outlet. The camping spot looks like it's about as quiet a place as it's possible to find for pitching a tent or having a picnic. On a late July day, there were small fish jumping in the lake, and the bugs weren't aggressive.

The mountainside— that of Bald Mountain— makes a fine backdrop to the lake. It is like many others along the Motorway: light-colored rock, dark green evergreen trees, low bushes, and grass. In the spring and summer, there would be a full palette of greens. In the fall, tan and red would replace some of the greens. No matter the season, the

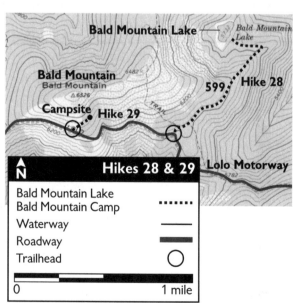

lake is an inviting spot.

Note: Some maps available over the internet show two trails down to the lake that are numbered 599. On the most recent maps available in 2001, the westernmost trail is the correct one (the one that starts at the tight corner).

Several species of huckleberry (*Vaccinium*) are found in this area. All have berries, though not all of the berries are blue. And all have urn-shaped flowers in shades of white to pink. The following are most common in this area.

The grouse whortleberry (*Vaccinium scoparium*) is the easiest to identify. It is a common, short understory plant at higher elevations, such as along the Motorway, and it actually looks a bit more like a small broom than a huckleberry. The plant is 4 to 10 inches tall, with $1/2$ inch slender yellow-green leaves. It blooms between May and August, and it bears a bright red, 3-to-5-millimeter berry in the fall, as early as August.

Dwarf huckleberry (*V. caespitosum*) is a 6- to 12-inch-high deciduous shrub with shiny leaves up to $1^1/2$ inches long and half as broad. They are toothed around the edges toward the tip. The berries of *V. caespitosum* are blue, with a white bloom that looks like dust on the outside.

Blue or globe huckleberry (*V. globulare*) is a 1- to 3-foot spreading deciduous shrub with 1 to $1^1/2$ inch long oval leaves. The flowers on this species are chubby, wider than they are long, and the berries are bluish purple with a white bloom on the outside. This species grows in the same ecological habitat as the big huckleberry or thin-leaf blueberry (*V. membranaceum*), also a spreading 1- to 3-foot deciduous shrub. *Vaccinium membranaceum* has 1 to 2 inch long oval leaves with pointed tips. This species is from a wet, more coastal environment. The pointed leaf tips are called "drip tips," and they shed the constant rain. The berries of *V. membranaceum* are purple or dark purplish red. *Vaccinium globulare* and *V. membranaceum* sometimes hybridize.

The western huckleberry (*V. occidentale*) lives in cold, wet, subalpine locations, at 6,000 feet or above in this area.

Deer and elk eat the leaves and tender shoots of the huckleberries, and the berries of all are eaten by grouse, rodents, marten, coyotes, and many other birds and mammals, including people, when they are lucky enough to find them. They are a staple food for black and grizzly bears, and one individual of the latter species can eat up to 70,000 berries in one day. The berries ripen first on the lower slopes, sometimes as early as the first of July, and the wave of ripening moves up the slopes, closely followed by the bears.

Years with poor berry crops can lead to serious problems, especially for black bear, as they search for the food they need to get through the winter's hibernation. That search often means increased human contact, always a bad deal for bears. (A reminder: we have only the black bears in this area at the time of this writing.

Beargrass (*Xerophyllum tenax*) looks like several things in addition to what it is, a member of the lily family. One early botanist thought it a yucca, and others, obviously, thought it was a grass.

Beargrass forms dense, evergreen clumps of grasslike leaves about 12 inches tall but larger than that in diameter. The top sides of the leaves are green while the undersides have fine white grooves. The plant flowers during the late summer but only sporadically, perhaps as seldom as once every five to seven years. The creamy white flowers are borne in a conical raceme (evenly spaced small flowers on a stem, with the bottom flowers opening first) at the end of 3- to 5-foot stalks. Should you happen to find a field with many in bloom, it's breathtaking.

The flowering stalks, flowers, and seed pods are eaten by a variety of small and large animals, but the leaves are unpalatable to all but the Rocky Mountain goat, historically plentiful in the area. Bears supposedly eat the early spring growth. Native Americans used the dried leaves for making clothing and fine baskets, while the roots were used for food. Some think Lewis and Clark named this plant "beard grass" because they thought it looked like the eastern Turkey beard grass.

Beargrass also is known as elkgrass, basket-grass, squawgrass, and bearlily.

Why: A short walk to a Lewis and Clark campsite and a small segment of the Nee-Me-Poo Trail.

Ease: Easy $\frac{1}{10}$ mile along a gentle uphill, a bit farther if you continue on the Nee-Me-Poo Trail.

Season: Mid-July through late September.

Maps: CWNF Visitor Map; USGS Holly Creek, Idaho. (The trail is not on either map.)

Information: North Fork Ranger District, CWNF, 208-476-4541.

Trailhead: On the right at mile 45.8 on the Motorway, across the road from the large brown sign commemorating Greensward Camp. (See page 120 for map.)

The Hike: Bald Mountain was a favorite camping place for most everyone who traveled the old Lolo Trail. It offered a warm, sunny and open, south-facing hillside in the spring and late fall, when other parts of the trail might still be under snow. There was ample grass and water for horses, as well as a beautiful resting place for the travelers.

Although aboriginal people probably camped at this location, the first written documentation of its use comes from the journals of Lewis and Clark. They camped here on June 26, 1806, on their eastbound journey. Lewis mentioned the abundance of beargrass, which the horses would not eat, and the abundance of other young and tender grasses, which they did eat.

Two ranger cabins were built near the creek at roughly the same site in the early days of the Forest Service, the first by Ranger Roy Monroe in 1910. The second, a larger cabin, was built near it in 1912 and used until 1927. The old horse and mule corrals were along the creek, to the east of the camp. Neither cabin survives today.

This is the only hike in the book that is not a forest service signed and maintained trail. It is included because of its history, because it is very short, and because it really would be difficult to lose your way between the road and the campsite.

There are tracks heading up the side of Bald Mountain from the road, parallel tracks about the size of those made by a pickup truck. Follow them to their end at a small, flat space that looks like a landing. That is where the campsite begins.

The campsite covered a large area, for there were about thirty people and their animals on the hillside when Lewis and Clark camped there that June night. It must have been a challenge to find a level sleeping spot.

The views from here are fine: Castle Butte with a lookout on top, No-see-um Butte, and the saddle between the latter and the ridge to its west. The combination of dark trees and green, subalpine meadows is quite picturesque.

Bald Mountain is covered with low vegetation, much of it beargrass, and a dotting of trees. When the beargrass is in bloom in early July, it's gorgeous. Continuing on uphill from the campsite for a few yards, you will find a trail tread that seems to follow a contour line along the hillside. Walk it for a bit. It is original, authentic, ancient Northern Nez Perce Trail. The best beargrass bloom is found by following this trail across a small creek to the east and on to the next hillside. The first year I visited the Motorway, it was covered with blooming beargrass, and the sky above was bright blue dotted with large, puffy white clouds.

Why: Excellent views after a short hike to the top of the ridge above No-see-um meadows.

Ease: Moderate to strenuous depending on how far you hike. The ridgetop is just $\frac{1}{2}$ mile in length and 300 feet up from the trailhead, and it continues for another gently undulating mile or so. No-see-um Butte is 4 miles from the trailhead with a 900-foot elevation gain and 1,500-foot loss over some of the ugliest trail I've hiked anywhere.

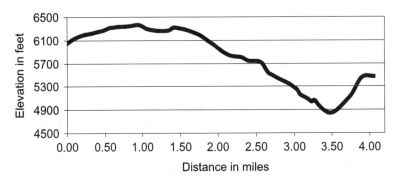

Season: Mid-July through late September.

Maps: CWNF Visitor Map; USGS Liz Butte, Idaho.

Information: Lochsa Ranger District, CWNF, 208-926-4274.

Trailhead: On the left at mile 49.1 on the Motorway. Be careful when parking to leave enough room for cars to pass.

The Hike: The sign just after the trailhead reads that it is 4 miles to No-see-um Butte, but do not let that be a deterrent to taking a shorter trip up the ridge and along the three small rises that sit upon its top.

That short trip covers a broad and open ridge with small groves of lodgepole pine, mountain hemlock, and Engelmann spruce, with a low understory of beargrass and whortleberry. And it gives you views. From various points on the ridgetop there are as good views to the south of the Selway Crags as there are from any trail along the Motorway. Looking upriver along the Motorway ridge, there is Castle Butte with its lookout, Bald Mountain, and the Bald Mountain Creek drainage sloping away below, which is a bright green meadow dotted with dark green trees. Looking downriver, there is Sherman Peak right next door to the west. And farther away, the Nez Perce prairie.

It is definitely a great spot to take a picnic, even a family one, for the hike up to the ridge is not difficult and the pleasant meadow and views are decidedly worth the walk.

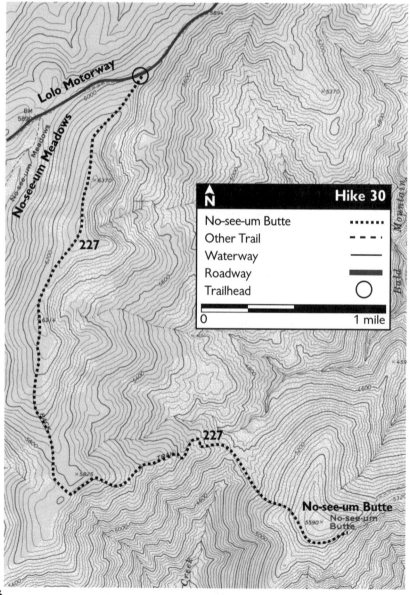

Hiking farther is another matter entirely. The trail leaves the ridgetop and heads down 500 feet of mostly steep, rocky, and skunky trail. Then it crosses a flat area where it can be hard to follow. By and large, it stays to the left side of the small ridge it follows through the flat. By and large, the trail is more worn, so it's lower and shows more dirt than nontrail. And by and large, it is pretty distinct everywhere except in one stretch, so it can be found with relative ease, even if you do lose it.

Once across the flat area, the trail again heads down, in a steep 1,000-foot drop to the saddle between the ridge the trail has just traveled and No-see-um Butte. This part of the trail is even uglier than the previous ugly section. The only positive thing to say about it is that it took less time coming back uphill than I thought it would, a very pleasant surprise.

From the saddle, which also separates the Bald Mountain and No-see-um Creek drainages, the views include the Lochsa Peak area, Coolwater Ridge, Castle Butte, and Bald Mountain—all visible during the first mile or so of the hike. It's an attractive spot but probably not worth the effort. Neither creek is available for refilling water bottles without hiking a fair bit down from the saddle.

I didn't hike the remaining $3/4$ mile of trail, with its 600-foot elevation gain, to the front of No-see-um Butte, but my hiking buddy did. He reported that although the trail up the Butte looks distinct from the saddle, it is overgrown in spots and can be hard to follow. The views are not as good as those from the ridgetop, the only reward being a glimpse of a tiny segment of the Lochsa River. The Forest Service says that the trail beyond that point is used and maintained primarily by outfitters.

I hiked this trail during the summer of 2000. My buddy and I enjoyed the views from the ridgetop, which also included a glimpse of the Camas Prairie to the southwest. When I sent my draft of this hike to Steve for checking, he corrected it, crossing out the views of the prairie and noting that it couldn't be seen from here. Previous work has always listed Sherman Peak as the easternmost spot from which it could be seen.

I replied that I was sure I had seen flat land, and the upshot was a July 4, 2001, evening hike up to the ridgetop for both of us. We took supper to eat while waiting for dark. We saw lights at exactly the compass reading for Grangeville. Binoculars showed the town even better, its streets laid out as expected. Even a few colorful fireworks. The autumn after this outing I also saw the Camas Prairie from Castle Butte.

Why: History and views. Sherman Peak is where some researchers think that Lewis and Clark saw their first glimpse of the Nez Perce Prairie to the west and southwest of them and realized their 1805 journey west through "those terrible mountains" would actually end.

Ease: Moderately easy. Although it is about 1 mile in length and an approximate 700-foot elevation gain from the trailhead to the top of the peak, the grade is surprisingly moderate. While the hike is not exactly easy, most people should be able to do it, if they take enough time.

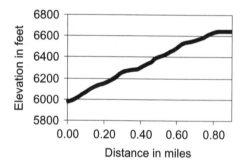

Season: Mid-July through late September.

Maps: CWNF Visitor Map; USGS Liz Butte, Idaho.

Information: North Fork Ranger District, CWNF, 208-476-4541.

Trailhead: The trailhead for FS#12 is on the left at mile 51.0 on the Motorway. It connects with the trail to Sherman Peak in about 1/3 mile.

The Hike: Sherman Peak also is called Spirit Revival Ridge, but there still is some discussion as to whether it actually was the first place from which Lewis or Clark saw the Nez Perce Prairie. If either did go up to the peak, it is probable he did so because every high spot was used as a means of getting better views of the country to the west.

The Clark party saw the prairie on the same day that they left the camp at Indian Grave and separated from Lewis. The Lewis party saw it the next day. There is no way to know whether the two men saw the prairie from the same place, and Steve always has suspected that they did not.

From the journal distances, Castle Butte and the trail to No-see-um Butte are unlikely first viewing spots, for the Corps camped after Castle Butte and at or after the No-see-um Butte trail before they saw the prairie. The distances reported in the journals make Willow Ridge or Bowl Butte most likely, and Steve's research places the location at Bowl Butte.

Sherman Peak was noted in the journals of most people who traveled the ancient Lolo Trail, although the main trail did not cross over the peak but went around on the north side as does the road. The surveyor for the Bird-Truax Trail was guided along the Lolo Trail in 1866, on a route that also went around the north side of Sherman Peak, not over it. That route is most likely the same as that traveled by Lewis and Clark. The trail to the peak itself probably started as a horse trail used by hunters that was augmented by subsequent visitors to the peak.

Sherman Peak and surrounding areas have been heavily scarred by fire during the past century, and some places still show rocks glazed by fire. Because the fires generally kept the peaks and ridges clear of trees, early travelers to Sherman Peak must have had spectacular, 360-degree views. Modern fire suppression has resulted in the tree growth that now partially obscures those views and will do so to a greater degree as the trees continue to grow.

The Bird-Truax Expedition called this peak Mt. Henderson, and it is not known when the name was changed to Sherman Peak.

An aboriginal trail to the north from the saddle on the west side of the peak was overlaid by the road that now goes out to the old lookout site at Liz Butte.

The connector trail heads uphill from the road, past a trail sign indicating that it is 1 mile to Sherman Peak. It passes through low brush for $^1/_4$ mile, until it meets the trail to the peak. Except for a few washouts along the way, it and the trail to the peak are in excellent condition.

The trail to the peak is relatively easy to walk, for it is essentially all switchbacks except for the steep, last few yards. On the top, however, it becomes indistinct, so mark your entry spot at least visually so it will be easier to find on the way down.

On the way up, the trail passes through moderately tall evergreens with a low understory that is primarily huckleberry. The peak has fewer trees,

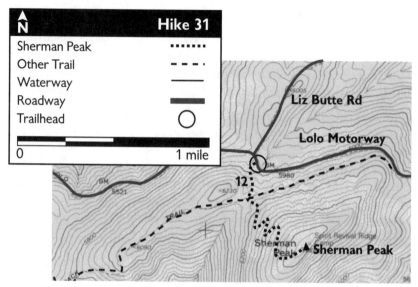

primarily in small groves of mountain hemlock and Engelmann spruce, rather than the scattered lodgepole pine that dominated the trip up.

Although they are not big, the trees on top still make it difficult to see all the views without moving around—a lot. And that situation is likely to get worse, for the trees will grow. I found a difference in just one year, between 2000 and 2001. But moving around the top will provide views. The Selway Crags to the south. Pot Mountain with Cook and Lookout Mountains to the north, as well as Windy Ridge, which connects the Motorway with the Cook and Lookout Mountain area. Liz Butte with the wonderful meadows on Weitas Ridge to its west. No-see-um Butte next door on the east, on the other side of an unnamed ridge, and on the west side, Weitas and Little Weitas Buttes and Rocky Ridge. And the Nez Perce Prairie in the distance to the west and southwest, of course. (Climbing on the rocks at the west edge of the peak helps with seeing in that direction.) On the way down there is also a fine view of Willow Ridge to the west.

Pot Mountain (seen from this hike and several others) was originally named "Piss Pot" by miners. There is a glacial cirque on the northeast side of it, a hollow that looks like a pot.

Connections: The FS#12 trail connects with the joint trail FS#25 and #40 (two sections of hike 40) at the saddle below Sherman Peak, first with the trail coming in from the east and then, at the same spot where it connects with the trail up to the peak, with the trail heading west. These trail junctions are to be signed but were not in 2001.

Liz Butte Trail FS#649 in combination

with FS#174 (Weitas Creek) and FS#650
(Yocum Creek)

Why: The hike visits a quiet, beautiful section of Weitas Creek and Liz Creek Cabin, plus it is the only hike from the Motorway with a circular portion.

Ease: Strenuous, 10 miles round trip with a 2,400-foot elevation change. I recommend hiking the circular section in a counterclockwise direction.

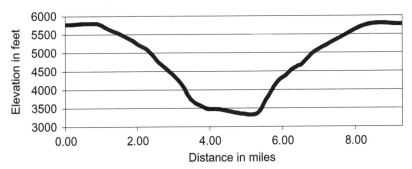

Season: Mid-July through late September.

Maps: CWNF Visitor Map; USGS Liz Butte, Idaho. (Both maps show a different trailhead location and initial ¾ mile of trail than is actually seen on the ground.)

Information: North Fork Ranger District, CWNF, 208-476-4541.

Trailhead: On the right, 1.5 miles up the road (#560) to Liz Butte, which is at mile 51.0 on the Motorway.

The Hike:

It was autumn the first time I hiked a portion of Weitas Creek. I started at its North Fork of the Clearwater River trailhead, where Weitas Creek ends. I was amazed that day to see bright red fish swimming upstream. I was new to the area and had no idea that there were such things as kokanee, or landlocked sockeye salmon.

Kokanee have been stocked into several areas in the region, after dams were built without accommodations for fish to move up and downstream. They must pass the dams if they are to breed and spend their early years in freshwater streams, yet travel to the ocean to grow into adulthood. Kokanee, however, grow to adulthood in freshwater, which is much less nutritious than the ocean. They mature at about 1 pound, while the ocean-maturing sockeye reach 7 to 14 pounds.

The sight of hundreds of them swimming upstream to spawn and die is still breathtaking.

The name "Weitas" is a euphemism for "Wet Ass," the original name of the creek. That name may have been coined by the soldiers in Howard's Nez Perce campaign or by the engineers laying road, though the latter also were known to have called it Huston Creek. Whichever is the case, the Forest Service changed the original "Wet Ass" to "Weitas," a more exotic but less expressive name.

The "Liz" of Liz Butte, Cabin, and Creek was a pack mule.

The route this trail follows is lollipop-shaped. It starts in a meadow at the trailhead mileage sign (Trail #650, 2 miles; Weitas Creek, 4 miles), and with a gradual downhill grade. Within a few minutes there are views of Castle Butte, with its lookout on top, and Bald Mountain. From then on, things alternate. The grade is sometimes moderate, sometimes flat, and sometimes steep, the latter especially the case when heading back to the trailhead at the end of the hike. The trail sometimes heads through meadows and some-times through woods of tall, two-foot or more in diameter trees. The only meadow where the trail is less than easy-to-see is on #649 soon after its junction with #650. Stay to the left in that meadow, and look for the blaze on the tree to the right of where the trail enters the next wooded area.

The signed junction of trails #649 and #650 is two miles from the trailhead, as posted. Continuing on #649 or the right fork, the trail passes through country similar to what it has already except the trees become a bit bigger, large cedar snags start to appear, and, at least in spots, the grade gets a lot steeper. The tread also is narrower and slants to the outside over the last half mile or so.

A sign at Weitas Creek points right to Liz Creek Cabin, a short side trip of $1/_{10}$ mile upstream and across Liz Creek via a wide, flat log bridge. The log

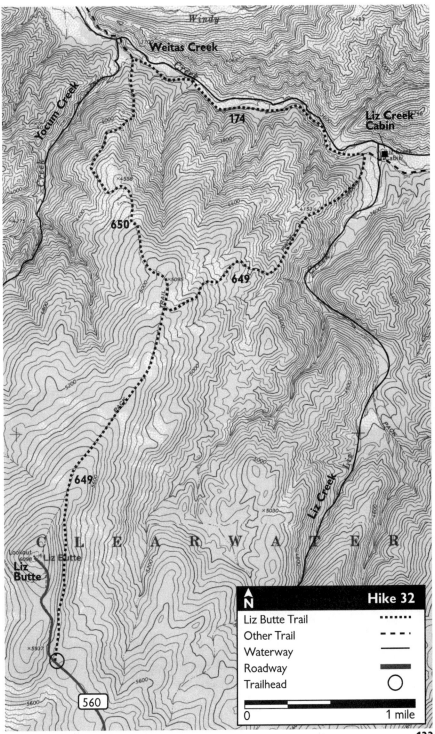

Liz Butte Trail

Hike 32
Liz Butte Trail ....
Other Trail ─ ─ ─
Waterway ────
Roadway ━━━━
Trailhead ◯

0 ━━━━━━━ 1 mile

cabin is picturesque, though in need of repair. Over the years it has served as a shelter for fire and trail crews.

To continue along the hike, turn left at Weitas Creek. The two miles of trail along the creek are relatively level and by far the most enjoyable part of the hike, at least on brutally hot July days. Often the creek splits into as many as three flat, rippling strands as it wends its way toward its junction with Windy Creek at the Upper Weitas Pack Bridge. Weitas Creek always looks clear, which probably accounts for the good western slope cutthroat fishing that can be found along its banks.

Although the trail does not go near the creek along those 2 miles, there are several places to filter water if necessary, or to cool off before the uphill hike. Three small side streams cross the trail along those 2 miles, and the trail goes down to Weitas Creek at a bridge that crosses it a few yards past where FS#650 heads uphill to the left.

Hiking uphill on trail FS#650 is just that: hiking uphill. There are switchbacks, something not much in evidence on trail FS#649 on the way down. There are a few views—of the Weitas Creek drainage, a bit of Pot Mountain, and parts of Windy Ridge. The highlight is a large meadow with trees and ferns and huge, dark blue larkspur. And the high point for me on the hot July day I hiked it was just surviving the trip up, for that 2 miles contains 1,700 feet of the hike's total elevation gain. There were abundant seasonal wildflowers along all three trails, as many as there have been on any of the area hikes.

Connections: This circle hike includes part of FS#174, a 14.7-mile stretch of trail that follows Weitas Creek from 12-mile Saddle (see appendix) to the North Fork of the Clearwater River. This trail does offer some fine hiking, but it is open to motorized vehicles for several miles at both ends.

Why: This is the premier day hike for trees on the Motorway, and it has exceptional meadows.

Ease: Strenuous, with a 1,400-foot elevation loss and 300-foot gain in 4-plus miles, one way.

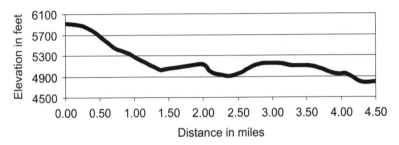

Season: Mid-July through late September.

Maps: CWNF Visitor Map; USGS Liz Butte, Idaho.

Information: North Fork Ranger District, CWNF, 208-476-4541.

Trailhead: On the left, 2 miles up the road to Liz Butte, which is at mile 51.0 on the Motorway.

The Hike: Except when it is in the meadows, the primary thing this hike provides is trees; even the meadows are framed by them. Though some trees are average in size, in many places there are specimens or groups of specimens that are 3 feet and more in diameter. There are huge Engelmann spruce, mountain hemlock, Douglas fir, grand fir, and larch—depending on where you are along the route. Walking through these stands of trees on a hot summer day makes it easy to appreciate not only their stature, age, and beauty but also the dense shade they provide. The patches of forests are markedly cooler than anyplace else.

Although this is a standard ridgeline trail of relatively short alternating ups and downs, the trail begins with one long, 1,000-foot downhill. Fortu-

Evergreen or needle trees: How to know what's what.

The following species are seen in the area covered by this book: Subalpine fir (*Abies lasiocarpa*), grand fir (*Abies grandis*), Douglas fir (*Pseudotsuga menziesii*), Engelmann spruce (*Picea engelmannii*), ponderosa pine (*Pinus ponderosa*), lodgepole pine (*Pinus contorta*), white pine (*Pinus monticola*), whitebark pine (*Pinus albicaulis*), mountain hemlock (*Tsuga mertensiana*), western hemlock (*Tsuga heterophylla*), Western red cedar (*Thuja plicata*), Pacific yew (*Taxus brevifolia*), and larch (*Larix occidentalis*).

Determining which is which can either be easy, if it is a ponderosa pine, western red cedar, or larch, or difficult, if it is any one of a number of the others. This is how I decide what I am looking at.

Pine trees usually have long needles in clusters, and there always are some needles on the ground under the tree to check. Ponderosa pine have wonderfully long needles, 5 to 8 inches long, in bunches of three. And its bark is distinctive, best described as orangy puzzle pieces with deep furrows. That it smells like vanilla or caramel or chocolate if you stick your nose in a furrow is only an extra benefit. (The exact smell seems to depend on the individual doing the smelling.)

Lodgepole pines are tall and narrow, with two needles in a bunch. (Hold up a thumb and first finger to make an "L" for lodgepole—two fingers, two needles, a lodgepole.)

White pines have needles in bunches of five, as do whitebark pines. But white pines have long, slender cones of 5 to 15 inches, and the bark is arranged in small, dark gray squares. Whitebark pines have shorter, stiffer needles, 2- to 4-inch cones, lighter bark in gray and/or brown, and in the area covered by this book, they grow only above elevations of about 5,000 feet.

Everything else has short needles except for cedars. Cedars are distinctive in that their needles are arranged in a fernlike manner, and their gray bark is in long strips, sometimes with red undertones.

Look up. It is a hemlock if the leader or highest branch droops to one side rather than standing up tall and straight. (I've read that the leader always points east.) Both types of hemlock also have needles of varying lengths. The western hemlock has small cones, less than 1 inch long, and the mountain hemlock has 1- to 3-inch cones. The western has a relatively flat needle arrangement on the stems, while the mountain has needles arranged radially around the stems, almost in little tufts. The mountain hemlock, also known as the black hemlock, is the one seen along the Motorway.

If the leader is straight and it is a tall tree, it is either a larch, a Douglas fir, a true fir, or a spruce.

Larch are distinctive in that their needles grow in tufts and they are deciduous, shedding the needles in the winter. The bark of the mature larch resembles that of the ponderosa pine.

The cones of a Douglas fir are characteristic. There are three-part bits that stick out from between some of the scales. A story about that: It seems that the Creator got mad at mice because they were so greedy. So, he stuck them in the cones, and you can still see them today, with their tails and back legs sticking out (the three bits). The bark on a mature Douglas fir also is very thick and dark with irregular deep furrows that often show orange to red color at their deepest part.

Cones from a true fir are rarely found on the ground, whether subalpine or grand (also known as white) fir. They disintegrate on the tree. Seen while still on the tree, they sit upright and only on branches near the top of the tree. Fir needles are flat, hard to roll between the fingers. And the needle arrangements tend to be soft, "You can shake hands with a fir but not with a spruce." Grand fir has a fairly uniform shape to the tree and its bark is light colored, with some dark or ashy brown, and deep furrows in the mature trees. The needles of the grand fir grow on a flat plane while those of a subalpine grow around the stem about half way.

Mature subalpine fir are very thin in overall shape and pointed at the top. They grow at higher elevations, and their bark is thin, gray, and smooth with blisters and shallow fissures.

The Engelmann spruce has cones, small ones 1 to 2 inches long, and the cones hang down from branches all the way up and down the tree. The bark is scaly and dark brownish red. The needles are round and can be rolled between the fingers.

And that brings us to the yew. It is a small tree in comparison to the rest, growing in the understory. In comparison to a fir or spruce of the same size, it has a messy growth pattern, and its bark is peeling.

nately, water crosses this section three times, so on the way back up to the trailhead there is ample opportunity to cool off.

Once past that downhill and on the ridgeline, the trail alternates between those wonderful, cool wooded areas and a series of meadows. Some of the meadows are small, just pockets of open space in the trees. Others

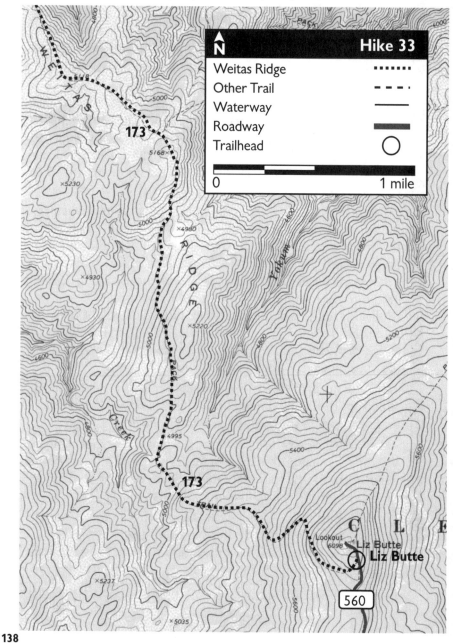

are large, especially one that is 3 to 4 miles into the hike. It is huge and grassy, maybe a quarter of a mile across, and is surrounded by trees and dotted with the flowers of summer, primarily bright red Indian paintbrush in mid-July. Other meadows have more flowers, with the red sometimes accented by companions in blue or yellow. And some offer better views: Liz Butte, Pot Mountain, Weitas and Little Weitas Buttes, Chimney Butte, or Rocky Ridge and Willow Butte.

But the views and the flowers are not the primary reason for hiking here, for better views can be seen on the Motorway with less effort, and easier spots can be found for viewing flowers. This hike is for the trees and for the meadows. It's for taking a picnic and sitting in that huge meadow— you'll know it when you get there. It makes a good turnaround spot, too. There are several more meadows in the next half mile or so, but the trail seems to disintegrate beyond that point.

There is a faint side trail off to the right of the main trail about 2 miles in, and when hiking out there is a faint trail visible off to the other side just before the final uphill. In addition, the trail can be indistinct through some of the meadows, and it might take a bit of work to follow it through and to the other side. Take a little extra time and carefully note the spot where the trail leaves the woods to enter each meadow.

There is one exception that might take a bit more time unless it has been cleared. About 2 miles into the hike there is a meadow where a downed tree lay on the first few feet of trail as it left the woods. From east to west, the trail heads to the right as it leaves the woods, and then to the left of two large fir. Then it is distinct through a patch of ferns and trees, heading to the right of a couple of big spruce. It then heads to the left of a patch of elderberries and to the right of a clump of larkspur as it passes around bushes that have overgrown the tread. From there, it is faint but visible through another open section, trees, and then ferns.

There is also a fork in the huge meadow that is most visible on your way back to the trailhead. Take the left.

Connections: The trail is listed as continuing for a total of 10.3 miles to Little Weitas Creek. In 2001, however, it disappeared about $1/2$ mile beyond the large meadow.

Why: The best views from a Motorway hike of Pot Mountain and the North Fork area of the Clearwater National Forest.

Ease: Moderate, with a 1,000-foot elevation gain in the first 1½ miles of this 2½-mile hike.

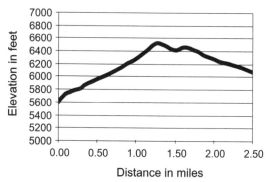

Season: Mid-July through late September.

Maps: CWNF Visitor Map; USGS Weitas Butte, Idaho.

Information: Lochsa Ranger District, CWNF, 208-926-4274.

Trailhead: On the left at mile 55.3 on the Motorway. Parking at this trailhead is poor. Keeping in mind that a full-sized pickup might pass by while you're there, it's best to park in a slightly wider spot to the east or west of the trailhead.

The Hike: There is a sign just after the start of the Willow Ridge Trail indicating that the trail ends in 4 miles. That was not the case in the year 2000, and it probably has not been for some time, for the trail has not been maintained for many years beyond a large meadow about 2½ miles in. Luckily, the great views that make this hike worthwhile come well before that, within the first mile.

The hike uphill to the top of Willow Ridge is steep at times, less so at others, with a couple of long switchbacks. Some sections are washed out, with many exposed roots. But it is not a difficult mile or so up to the edge of the ridgeline, where there are views of not only the North Fork but also into the Willow Creek drainage between Willow Ridge and Sherman Peak. The former can be seen without going that far, but the latter make the slightly longer hike worth doing.

The Willow Creek drainage is a lovely, treed bowl. Lewis and Clark passed by it in 1805 as they made their way from Sherman Peak over the northern end of Willow Ridge and toward Bowl Butte. Steve's research suggests that they came up the ridgeline from Sherman Saddle, passed not far from where you may be sitting to enjoy the view, and headed down into Deep Saddle and over Bowl Butte. Others think they went down Willow Ridge along this hiking trail and its continuation to, and then up, Hungery Creek.

Kinnikinnick (*Arctostaphylos uva-ursi*) is a member of the heath family, and the last part of its name means "bears' grape." It is a common prostrate, low-growing evergreen plant with small, leathery, dark green oval leaves that are a bit shiny. The plant blooms between March and June, with small, pink, urn-shaped flowers in terminal clusters or racemes. The bright red berries remain on the plant over the winter, are edible though tart if eaten raw, and make a good jelly.

The name kinnikinnick is aboriginal, meaning "mixture," and was usually applied to any smoking mix. Native Americans used the plant's leaves for tobacco, to make tea, or as a yellow dye. The tannin in the leaves can be used to cure hides.

The leaves and twigs are eaten by deer and mountain sheep during the fall and winter, and the berries are eaten by black bears, rodents, and various birds.

Kinnikinnick grows on dry open exposures, often in association with ponderosa pines, and is found throughout the northern hemisphere.

In the North Fork, Pot Mountain is unmistakable, a huge rock edifice that seems divided into two segments. In front of Pot Mountain there is the closer Rocky Ridge, Weitas Butte with a lookout on top, and Little Weitas Butte with its rocky, south-facing slope. To the right of Pot Mountain, there are Cook and Lookout Mountains on the North Fork and a series of Motorway peaks: Bald Mountain, Chimney Butte with what looks like a pointed, gravel top, and Sherman Peak. The Selway Crags and the Bitterroot Divide are south of the Lochsa River.

It is about 2 miles to the top of Willow Ridge. I hiked another half mile or so beyond that, down a couple of hundred feet to where I lost the trail in the large grassy meadow that contains a huge campsite. I'm told that the trail—the part that's not maintained—stays to the east and above this meadow rather than entering it, and though I searched that area for signs of it, I had no luck.

There is a faint fork in the trail about 2 miles in, but the left "fork" is obviously the trail. There probably was a rerouting, for a faint trail seems to rejoin the main trail from the right a short time later. In 2000, the brush along much of the trail was close enough that when it was wet, pantlegs were wet, too.

Connections: Shortly after the 4-mile sign at the start of the hike, this trail crosses the FS#40 trail. In this area, FS#40 runs from Sherman Saddle to Deep Saddle (hike 40c) and from Sherman Saddle to this trail junction, FS#25 is contiguous with FS#40.

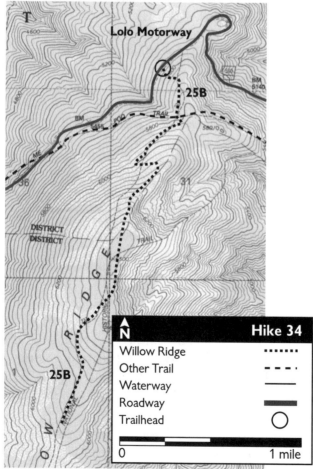

N	Hike 34
Willow Ridge	•••••••
Other Trail	- - - ·
Waterway	——
Roadway	▬▬
Trailhead	○

0   1 mile

Rocky Ridge Lake Overview Trail FS#40C

Why: Excellent views into the Clearwater National Forest.

Ease: Easy, short, three-minute walk.

Season: Mid-July through late September.

Maps: CWNF Visitor Map; USGS, Weitas Butte, Idaho. (The trail is not on the latter.)

Information: North Fork Ranger District, CWNF, 208-476-4541.

Trailhead: The trailhead is on the right at mile 63.8 on the Motorway.

The Hike: Rocky Ridge Lake has been a popular camping spot for decades. Once the Lolo Motorway was completed in 1934 and easy access became possible, the lake became a summer weekend getaway for nearby residents.

The trail from the Motorway to the overview was constructed in the early 1990s as part of "Take Pride in America," a program that encouraged participation in public service projects. It began as a federal program but was continued for many years by the CWNF because it was well supported locally.

Popular folklore says there are army cannons at the bottom of Rocky Ridge Lake dating from the 1877 Nez Perce War. General O. O. Howard and the United States Army pursued the nontreaty Nez Perce from Whitebird, Idaho, to north of the Bear Paw Mountains in Montana, just shy of the Canadian border. The folklore says that the army tired of carrying the cannons over the Lolo Trail and abandoned them in the lake so that the Nez Perce would not be able to make use of them. That a cannon ball or two has been reported along the trail only fuels the folklore.

Steve's favorite tale relating to the folklore includes the building of a raft that was taken out on the lake by people hunting for cannons. The occupants of the raft thought they saw a cannon at the bottom of the lake, so they went back to shore and located some old number nine telephone wire. They failed in their attempt to fish out the cannon using the wire. The raft broke apart, they abandoned their efforts, and never came back to try again.

The trail heads off to the right of the trailhead sign, and it is level and easy to follow all the way to where it overviews Rocky Ridge Lake and a large sweep of the Clearwater area, from Pot Mountain on the North Fork around to Sherman Peak on the Motorway. Using a CWNF Visitor Map positioned to align with the lake and Weitas Butte (about 3 miles away, treed, and with a lookout on top), it is possible to identify Pot Mountain (huge and rocky), Little Weitas Butte, Cook Mountain, the Moose Creek Buttes, Scurvy Mountain, Sherman Peak, Castle Butte (topped by a lookout), and Bald Mountain (treed on the north side, relatively open on the south, with a road cut).

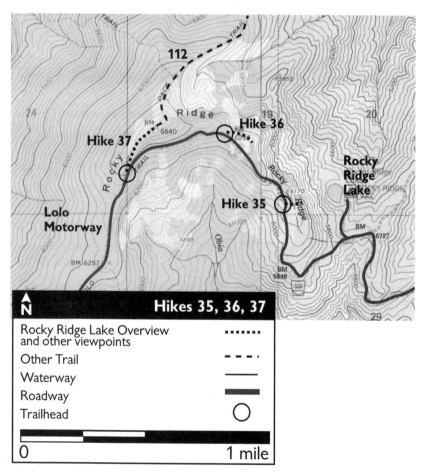

Why: Fine views from a site that sits just above the Nee-Me-Poo Trail.

Ease: Easy, less than $1/_{10}$ mile of moderate uphill.

Season: Mid-July through late September.

Maps: CWNF Visitor Map; USGS Snowy Summit, Idaho. (The trail is not on either, however.)

Information: North Fork Ranger District, CWNF, 208-476-4541.

Trailhead: On the right at mile 64.4 on the Motorway. (See page 144 for map.)

The Hike: The trailhead is marked by a historic trail marker a few yards back from the Motorway, but the trail to the viewpoint is actually above the Nee-Me-Poo Trail. The latter runs below the knoll.

There is a double track from the marker to the viewpoint at the top of the small knoll that sported a small rock pile in 2001. With a CWNF Visitor Map, it is possible to identify a great deal of what can be seen, both from this knoll and the next one over. Pot Mountain, that large rock edifice, and the ridges and peaks of the Mallard-Larkins roadless area are to the northwest. Beyond them is a picture postcard of ridgeline after ridgeline, the colors fading in proportion to the distance.

Walking farther, in the same general direction that the tracks would have taken had they continued beyond the knoll, brings more views. Just guide toward the distant hill with a couple of bare spots, and you will come to the second knoll a hundred or so yards farther on, behind a bunch of small trees and bushes. From there, it is possible to see everything from the east side of Pot Mountain through the North Fork Clearwater River area to the expanse of the Motorway ridge. On the other side of the Lochsa River, there are Grave Peak, the Selway Crags, and Chimney Peak. Outstanding views for little effort.

Note: This site, as well as that of the nearby Rocky Ridge Lake Overview, may be included on a major Nee-Me-Poo Trail reroute. Check with the CWNF for information.

Why: A short and easy uphill walk to good views.

Ease: Easy, less than $1/2$ mile in length and a 200-foot elevation gain.

Season: Mid-July through late September.

Maps: CWNF Visitor Map; USGS Snowy Summit, Idaho. (The latter shows the trail continuing past the lookout site, but it has not been maintained beyond the lookout for several years.)

Information: North Fork Ranger District, CWNF, 208-476-4541.

Trailhead: On the right at mile 65.0 on the Motorway. (See page 144 for map.)

The Hike: The trail follows the old road up to the site of an old lookout. There's not much to see along the way, but the view from the top makes up for that. Huge and rocky Pot Mountain dominates the North Fork of the Clearwater. A look at a map shows its size in another way, for the North Fork of the Clearwater River and the road along it make a huge detour around the mountain's base. The Mallard-Larkins roadless area is northwest of Pot, a series of gentle and slightly sloping peaks and ridges. Unfortunately, the alpine lakes and mountain goats that attract people to the area aren't seen from this far away.

The Selway Crags are close, visible from between the trees on the south side of the clearing. And going a few yards farther down the trail past the old sign at the north edge of the clearing provides some views of the Cook and Lookout Mountain area between the Motorway and the North Fork of the Clearwater River.

I have not seen bitterroot (*Lewisia rediviva*) in the area that is covered by this book, but I have included it lest you think I had forgotten the flower named for Lewis. He collected it in 1806 in Montana and sent it back East. Months later, one of his dried specimens revived when planted, hence rediviva, meaning "restored to life."

The bitterroot flower is quite shocking, a 1 to 2 inch, deep pink to white "water lily" that sits almost directly on the bare, dry ground, the leaves having already sprouted and withered away.

Bitterroot was considered a valuable plant by Native Americans. They dug the roots in early spring, before the plants flowered and when the roots were tender and still held starches. They usually boiled or baked them or dried them to store for winter use. The roots taste bitter when raw, especially after the spring, hence its common name, and Lewis and Clark thought it tasted bitter even when prepared.

Bitterroot is the state flower of Montana and all the other bitterroots (mountains, valley, etc.) are named after it.

Why: A short hike to the Lewis and Clark campsite known as Horsesteak Meadows, which sits beside a gorgeous, pristine creek.

Ease: Easy, ½ mile in length and 240-foot elevation loss down to the campsite, with another ½ mile of level trail along the creek.

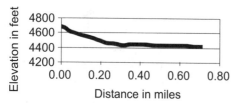

Season: Mid-July through late September.

Maps: CWNF Visitor Map; USGS Boundary Peak, Idaho, and Snowy Summit, Idaho. The latter shows the trail continuing uphill, but it is not maintained past the first creek crossing, and travel uphill on this section is strongly discouraged.

Information: Lochsa Ranger District, CWNF, 208-926-4274.

Trailhead: On the left at Windy Saddle, 3.9 miles up the road to Boundary Peak. That road is a left turn off the Motorway at mile 70.7.

The Hike:

The metal mileage markers on the trees that are found along some of the area's trails date from the 1930s. Steve's research suggests that the route of this trail down to the creek probably dates from the same time, as a means of access to the area for hunting, and that the trail did not exist when Lewis and Clark passed through this area.

Clark and his party found and killed a horse here after splitting from Lewis. They ate some and left the rest for Lewis and his group. Neither party camped here heading west, but the Corps did camp here on June 16, 1806, on their unsuccessful first trip east.

This hike is appealing even if its historical connection to Lewis and Clark is not of interest. The Hungery Creek drainage is a delight and well worth the short downhill hike, even worth the uphill hike back to the trailhead. Hungery Creek is as pristine a creek as can be imagined. It is clear, cold, and the slopes around it look like they have never seen commercial activity. In early July, the creek crossing was lined with tall magenta shooting stars. The grassy, wet meadows that fill the flat area in which the creek meanders were bright green. Trees line the trail, most of them Engelmann spruce, making it a good place to become familiar with that species' scaly bark. They are large trees, for the area escaped the fires of the early 1930s.

The meadows across the creek can be muddy and wet. In early July, it was drying out in most spots, but in one still-damp area, I found a distinct cougar track. In the next such area, I found tracks of the same size and shape as well as smaller ones of the same shape. I'd like to think that a female and cub had passed by earlier that morning.

The trail heads uphill a bit past the metal 1-mile marker on a tree.

On the way down from the top, Bowl Butte is visible in the distance with Willow Ridge to its right. It's easy to see how the former was named when it's seen from this vantage point.

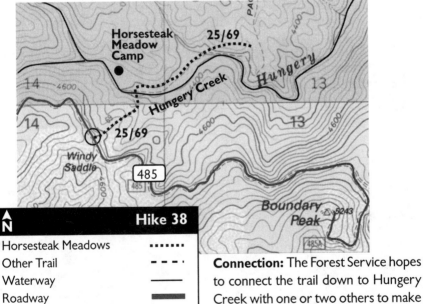

Hike 38

Horsesteak Meadows	·······
Other Trail	- - - ·
Waterway	——
Roadway	▬▬
Trailhead	○

0   .5 mile

Connection: The Forest Service hopes to connect the trail down to Hungery Creek with one or two others to make a circle hike. It should be a fine one.

Note: Just after the trailhead, there is a side trail off to a small meadow that sits below the trail.

Mex Mountain to the
Lolo Campground FS#25

This hike is composed of four segments, A–D. Each is listed individually below. The entire 14 miles is constructed along the same general route as that followed by Lewis and Clark both in 1805 and 1806.

The Corps of Discovery actually made four separate trips over this route, one while heading west in 1805, and three while heading east in 1806. There are four of its campsites along these trail segments.

During the westbound trip, Clark led a separate advance party, with Lewis and the main party two days behind. Clark camped at the Cedar Grove on September 19, 1805, and Lewis camped on the ridge above Salmon Trout

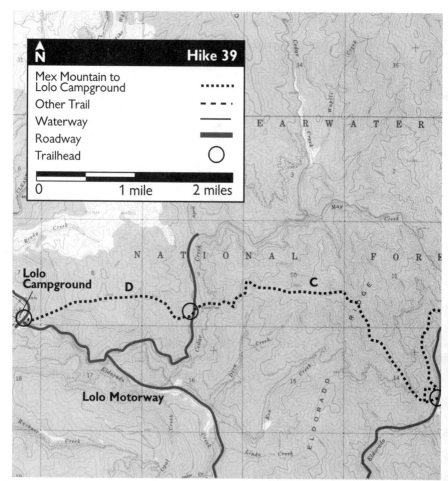

Camp on September 20, 1805.

In mid-June of 1806, the party made their first attempt at returning east. They camped at Small Prairie Camp on June 15 and at Horsesteak Meadow Camp on Hungery Creek the next night (see hike 38). On June 17, they were turned back by heavy snow southwest of Bowl Butte and retreated to Hungery Creek, camping below the mouth of today's Obia Creek. June 18 they retreated to Eldorado Creek and camped at Salmon Trout Camp until June 20, after which they returned to the Weippe Prairie. There they regrouped, resupplied, obtained Nez Perce guides, and waited for the snow to melt.

Their second—and successful—trip east began June 24. They camped that night at Salmon Trout Camp, and on Hungery Creek at Buffalo Robe Camp the following night.

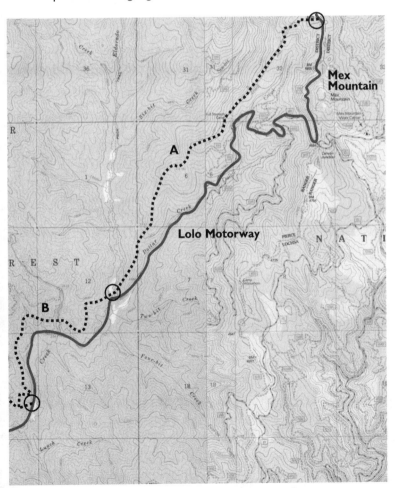

The areas adjacent to the trail have been heavily logged in the past, and many roads were constructed for timber harvest. Several of these are crossed by this trail. During the years of heavy timber harvest, the trail was little used, and few knew of this area's role in the journey of Lewis and Clark. Ralph Space is generally credited with making the public aware of the historical value of the trail and for preserving what remained of the route and its old-growth trees. He set aside the Cedar Grove and the Clark Tree area to prevent them from being logged. In his book *The Clearwater Story*, he tells of someone carving William Clark's initials on a tree in the area and then letting people think it was authentic.

A. Mex Mountain to Salmon Trout Camp

Why: Fine, large trees.

Ease: Moderate, 4-mile hike with a 1,200-foot elevation loss.

Season: June through late October.

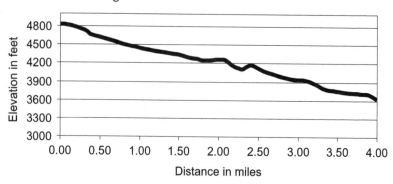

Maps: CWNF Visitor Map; USGS Musselshell and Boundary Peak, Idaho. (The trail is not on the current edition of either USGS map.)

Information: Lochsa Ranger District, CWNF, 208-926-4274.

Trailhead: The trailhead is at mile 75.2 on the Motorway. There is no parking at or near this trailhead as of this writing, although there are plans to clear space there for a couple of cars.

Unless the parking area is cleared, I do not recommend hiking it from this end. To reach the Salmon Trout Camp trailhead, drive 5.4 miles past the Mex Mountain trailhead, the equivalent of mile 79.6 on the Motorway, and turn right on the 524 Road. The signed trailhead is on the right a few feet up that road.

Alternately, to reach the Salmon Trout Trailhead from Kamiah, Idaho, turn east off of Highway 12 at the east end of the bridge over the Clearwater River, then turn right 0.4 miles later at the Forest Access sign. Stay right 1.2 miles farther. The road becomes gravel 10 miles from that point (unless it has since been paved by the county), but is paved again when you stay left at

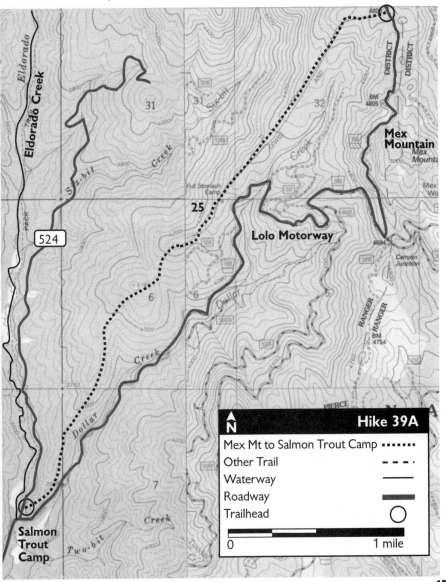

the "Y" 6 miles later. Turn right on to the 500 Road, which is another 6.2 miles later, just past the Lolo Campground. Turn left on the 524 Road 9.2 miles farther east, just after the 500 Road crosses the creek. The trailhead is on the right a few feet up that road.

The Hike: This section of trail is an easy, downhill hike. It is the best of the segments because it is a good combination of an open, low understoried forest with a wide variety of large trees, a fine selection of wildflowers in season, and enough filtered sunlight to provide warmth on a cool day. Even when hiked from the bottom, it seems easier than it might, for the uphill stretches don't seem long until the trail nears Mex Mountain.

Once past the trail sign, which is a few yards in from the Lolo Motorway trail marker, the trail travels first through thimbleberry and other moderately sized brush, then passes a spring on the right after $1/3$ mile. There are occasional boulder outcrops for the first mile, and trees throughout, the hike. The biggest are grand fir, Douglas fir, Western red cedar, ponderosa pine, and white pine. In the year 2000, the many downed trees seemed to equally represent all of these species except cedar. Almost no cedar were down.

As the trail continues downhill, the understory gets lower and the cedar become more numerous. The trail alternates between both sides of the ridge, and there are occasional peeks through the trees. But frankly, there's not much to see. This section is blazed all the way, and there are no roads and no side trails.

B. Salmon Trout Camp to Small Prairie Camp via the connector trail FS#14

Why: Level trail with fine wildflowers in season.

Ease: Easy $2^1/3$ miles of essentially level trail.

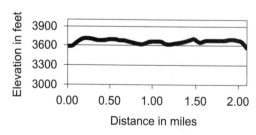

Season: May through late October.

Maps: CWNF Visitor Map; USGS Musselshell, Idaho. (The trail is not on the current edition of the latter.)

Information: Lochsa Ranger District, CWNF, 208-926-4274.

Trailhead: The trailhead is on the right at mile 79.6 on the Motorway, at the sharp corner just past the bridge. From Kamiah, the trailhead is on the left at 9.2 miles along the 500 Road.

The Hike: When I hiked this trail in early July, there were fields of creamy white false hellebore in bloom in the low areas along Eldorado Creek. Their breathtaking beauty was visible while driving to the trailhead and while hiking the first few yards along the connector.

This section feels more open than the others, and some of that feeling may be due to the trail's proximity to the 500 Road and the resultant lack of nearby canopy cover. In general, it also seems less used, narrower, and less uniform than the other sections. It's worth walking for the woods and the wide selection of wildflowers, though the road crossings detract from the overall experience.

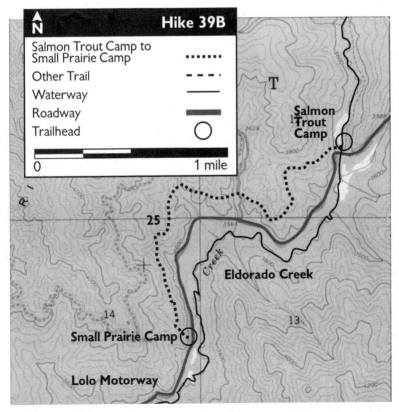

The trail is slightly uphill for $1/2$ mile until it goes straight across a road. Although the trail is signed on both sides of the road, one of the posts was missing its sign in 2000. Once across the road, the trail continues to the left at the back of the open area, then switchbacks down to cross another road a short distance later. From here on, the grade is level or moderate.

A couple of miles into the hike, there's a subtle change. The trail is still trail-width, but it's on a flat area that's wider than the trail and more open, with the larger trees farther back. The trail is on an old road bed.

The junction with the FS#25 trail up from Small Prairie Camp and toward the Lolo Campground is signed. Take a left to head down to Small Prairie Camp and the 500 Road, or continue ahead, up the ridge toward the Cedar Grove and the Lolo Campground.

Note: The connector trail does not follow the actual route of Lewis and Clark. Their route went through the neighboring swampy area along Eldorado Creek.

C. Small Prairie Camp to the Cedar Grove

Why: Fine large cedar and ponderosa pine.

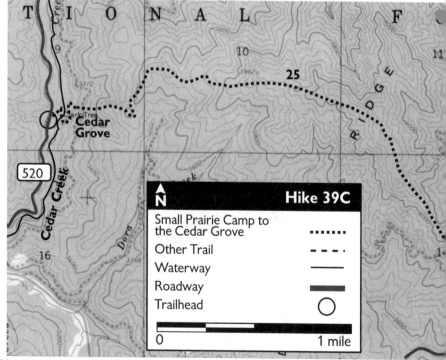

Ease: Moderate, a 4½-mile hike with a 500-foot elevation gain and an 800-foot elevation loss.

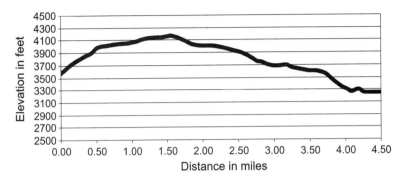

Season: May through late October.

Maps: CWNF Visitor Map; USGS Musselshell, Idaho. (Note: The trail is not on the current edition of the latter.)

Information: Lochsa Ranger District, CWNF, 208-926-4274.

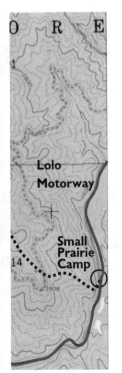

Trailhead: The trailhead is across the road from the Small Prairie Camp information sign at mile 81.3 on the Motorway. Coming from Kamiah, the trailhead is 7.5 miles along the 500 Road after the junction of the 500 and 100 Roads.

The Hike: The trail switchbacks up the hill from the trailhead sign to its junction with the connector, where the sign indicates the direction and mileage to the Small Prairie Camp (¼ mile), Salmon Trout Camp (3 miles), and the Cedar Grove (4 miles).

To head to the Cedar Grove, turn left at the junction sign, head uphill and be prepared to see almost every kind of tree in the area: Pacific yew, white pine, ponderosa pine, Engelmann spruce, Western red cedar and, most of all, grand fir, and Douglas fir.

The first road crossing comes in about ¾ mile. The trail continues straight across, but to find the section on the other side of the road, it is necessary to turn left and walk along the road for several yards. The trail sign is on the right, along with the trail heading up the hill.

After more uphill interspersed with a token downhill or two, and a couple of peeks through the trees at a distant prairie, the trail comes to a second road crossing. The trail on the other side is 25 yards to the right. It starts as an overgrown old road that is signed, "No mechanical vehicles." It soon becomes more trail-like, and after $1/4$ mile or so, there is a sign on the left with mileage to the Clark Tree ($2\frac{1}{2}$), Lolo Campground ($4\frac{1}{2}$), and Small Prairie Camp ($1\frac{3}{4}$). A second sign indicates that this section of trail is maintained by the Northwest Children's Home.

Another 2 miles of downhill hiking brings road crossing number three, which the trail goes straight across. During that 2 miles, the trail passes scattered superb and huge old ponderosa pines.

The Clark Tree is on a signed spur to the left off this trail a few yards later, and not much farther along, there is a bridge to the cedar grove. Take the left fork to continue hiking, or the right fork to head to the small parking lot and pit toilet.

There are huge cedars in the grove, up to 5 feet in diameter, so it's definitely worth a visit.

D. Cedar Grove to Lolo Campground

Why: Cedar and Pacific yew.

Ease: Moderate, $2\frac{1}{2}$-mile hike with a 250-foot elevation gain and a 600-foot elevation loss.

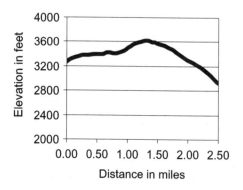

Season: May through late October.

Maps: CWNF Visitor Map; USGS Musselshell, Idaho. (Note: The trail is not on the current edition of the USGS map.)

Information: Lochsa Ranger District, CWNF, 208-926-4274.

Trailhead: Turn right on the 520 Road at mile 87.7 on the Motorway. The trailhead is on the left after 1¹/₂ miles, and a parking area and pit toilet are ¹/₁₀ mile farther along on the right. The cedar grove is on the right side of the road in the same place, and the trail toward Small Prairie Camp (hike C) heads through it.

From Kamiah, turn right on to the 500 Road just beyond Lolo Campground and drive 1.1 miles, then turn left on to the 520 Road.

To reach the Lolo Campground trailhead from Weippe, Idaho, drive east out of that town on Pierce Road. Its name will change to Musselshell Road. At mile marker 8, go straight, toward Musselshell as signed, and beyond for 9.5 more miles to the intersection of the 100 and 500 Roads.

The Hike: This section of the trail starts with a sign indicating that it is maintained by the Boy Scouts of America. It's probably not surprising, given the

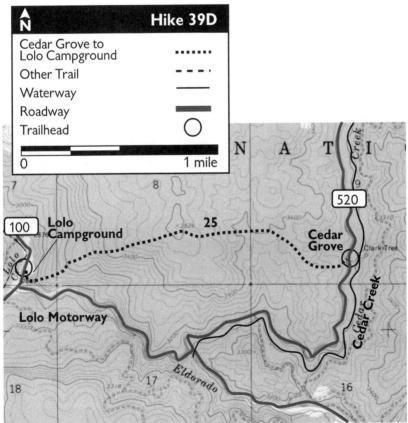

neighboring cedar grove, that the trail starts along a small drainage with big cedars along the trail. The farther it goes, the smaller the cedars will become, but they're always there. As they become less numerous, other tree species become more so.

One dark, mostly cedar area about mid-way through this hike holds some fine, large Pacific yew, 8 to 10 inches in diameter. They are lovely things, with their slightly unkempt growth habit making them an interesting contrast to the highly ordered fir trees of the same size.

After this section of trail tops out, it passes a couple of openings that provide views of a nearby ridge. The second opening has a mossy, rocky knoll that makes a comfortable resting spot. The hike ends with a few minutes of switchbacking down through the trees to the trailhead sign on the 100 Road.

The trail through this section seems to be the least used of all, maybe because if it is hiked from the campground, which is the easiest trailhead to reach, it's a long uphill pull to get anywhere.

Hike 40 is composed of eleven segments, A–K. Each is listed individually below. Trail #40 is the Forest Service designation for the Nee-Me-Poo or Nez Perce National Historical Trail that commemorates the 1877 Nez Perce War and the flight of the nontreaty Nez Perce from Wallowa Lake, Oregon, to the Bear Paw Mountains of Montana.

The 1,170-mile journey of the Nez Perce in 1877 was the only time this trail was used in its entirety. The component trails and roads had been used for generations before that, however, and have been used by the generations that have followed.

The Nez Perce originally was a collection of independent villages and bands that lived in southeastern Washington, northeastern Oregon, and north central Idaho. They lived simply: digging roots, fishing, and hunting. Their first known meeting with whites was on September 20, 1805—the day that William Clark and six others met them on the Weippe Prairie.

The Tribe welcomed Clark and his men, and they welcomed Meriwether Lewis and the rest of the Corps of Discovery when they stumbled out of the Bitterroot Mountains two days later. The men of the Corps were provided with much-needed food, camas and dried salmon, and they stayed with the Tribe for three weeks. When the Corps was ready to leave, Chief Twisted Hair gave them canoes and accompanied them halfway to the Pacific. The Nez Perce kept the Corps' horses during that winter. The Tribe believed the words of peace that Lewis and Clark spoke during their visit, and they have been friendly to whites from that time to the present.

The visit of Lewis and Clark was followed by the increased immigration of whites into the west. As a result, in 1855 Washington Territory Governor Isaac I. Stevens negotiated a treaty with the Nez Perce chiefs. It recognized the latter's right to their traditional homeland, establishing it as a reservation of about 5,000 square miles.

The treaty was like many others in that it was not to take effect until after it had been ratified by Congress and after the Nez Perce had received their first payment. Like many treaties before, the settlers came in long before ratification or payment. The area stayed peaceful, however, until 1860, when prospectors struck gold on the reservation. The gold rush that followed led to much of the reservation being overrun by thousands of whites.

The U.S. Government engaged the Nez Perce in new treaty talks at a large council in 1863, with most of the separate bands of the tribe represented. During the council, some bands became disgusted and left, refusing to cede their land. After their departure, the remaining chiefs did cede that land, though they lacked the authority to do so. The Nez Perce were left with just 700,000 acres. Chief Old Joseph, Chief Joseph's father, called this treaty the "thief treaty."

The now-divided tribe was composed of those who had signed the treaty, the "treaty" Nez Perce, and those who had not, the five "nontreaty" Nez Perce bands. The nontreaty bands continued to live on their lands for many years following the 1863 treaty, but conflicts with the growing white population increased, especially in Wallowa country, the homeland of Chief Joseph's band.

In May 1877, the remaining nontreaty Nez Perce were ordered to turn over their land to the whites and move to a small reservation in Lapwai, Idaho. Recognizing that no realistic alternative existed and hoping to avoid conflict, the nontreaty chiefs agreed to do so. Unfortunately, while they were en route to Lapwai, several young Nez Perce warriors rode out to the Salmon River. They killed several whites to avenge past murders of tribal members. Their actions were followed soon after by the Army's attack on the Nez

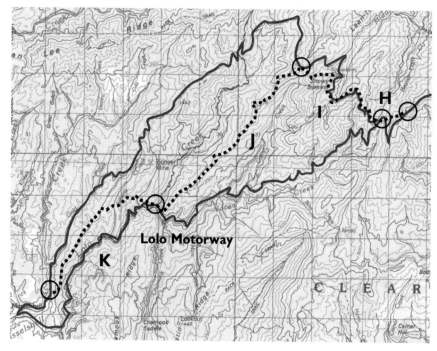

Perce at White Bird Canyon, Idaho, on June 17, 1877.

The 750 nontreaty Nez Perce (250 warriors plus women and children, the old and the sick, and 2,000 horses) left the White Bird area hoping to seek safety with their Crow allies on the plains. When that failed to occur, Canada became their last hope. Along their journey toward Canada they fought twenty battles and skirmishes against a total of more than 2,000 soldiers and volunteers. They were captured just shy of the Canadian border on October 5, 1877.

Little is known about their actual trip across the 25-plus miles of Nee-Me-Poo Trail that you can hike, from the Lolo Motorway east of Sherman Peak to the north end of Musselshell Meadows. It is certain that they camped at Weippe on July 15, 1877, and that they headed east on the Lolo Trail the following day, camping that night at Musselshell Meadows. They probably camped at Weitas Meadows during their trip, and they arrived at Fort Fizzle in Montana on July 26.

Your journey certainly will be easier. There are many trailheads along this section of trail, much of which is intertwined with the Motorway. All are marked with the historical signpost. Except for the miles from Musselshell to Willow Ridge, this route is the same as that followed by Lewis and Clark and largely the same route as that surveyed by the Bird-Truax Expedition.

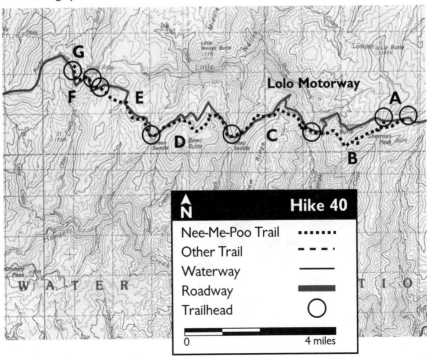

The Nee-Me-Poo Trail was dedicated in 1986. It is part of the national trail system and the only National Historic Trail that is administered by the Forest Service. As a National Historic Trail, all forms of mechanized travel, including pedal bicycles, are prohibited.

For more information, visit the Forest Service website: www.fs.fed.us/ r1/clearwater/nezpercenht/nezperce.htm.

There are several distinct sections to this 28-mile segment of the Nee-Me-Poo Trail from near Sherman Peak to Musselshell Meadows. Most are accessed from the Motorway, but the westernmost three sections can be reached from the west via Kamiah or Weippe, earlier and later in the season than the Motorway generally is open.

A. Motorway to FS#12

B. From FS#12 to Sherman Saddle

C. Sherman Saddle to Deep Saddle

D. Deep Saddle to Green Saddle

E. Green Saddle to Weitas Meadows

F. Motorway to Motorway

G. Rocky Ridge Overview to Motorway

H. Motorway to Beaver Dam Saddle

I. Beaver Dam Saddle to Camp Martin

J. Camp Martin to Lolo Forks

K. Lolo Forks to Musselshell Meadows

Note: At the time of hiking in 2000 and 2001, the trail from Weitas Meadows to Beaver Dam Saddle consisted of three disparate sections of hiking trail and several miles of Motorway walking. The CWNF hopes to reroute the Motorway sections so as to provide a more hiker-friendly experience. Check with the CWNF to determine whether this rerouting has been completed.

At this time, all Motorway intersections with the Nee-Me-Poo Trail are signed with a historic signpost: a vertical post with a slanted top and a white Nee-Me-Poo Trail triangle.

While hiking segments of this trail, whether for exercise, enjoyment, or history, please keep in mind that this trail is part of the history of the Nez Perce. The Tribe made an arduous, difficult journey over the route, and many have died along the route—then, before, and after. Please treat it with respect as you walk.

A. Motorway to FS#12

Why: Suitable for the family and good views.

Ease: Easy, ¾-mile trail with little elevation change.

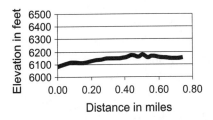

Season: Mid-July through late September.

Maps: CWNF Visitor Map; USGS Liz Butte, Idaho.

Information: Lochsa Ranger District, CWNF, 208-926-4274.

Trailhead: On the left at mile 50.4 on the Motorway.

The Hike: This is the most level bit of trail I've hiked off the Motorway, crossing just a couple of contour lines on the topographic maps (80 feet maximum elevation gain) over ¾ mile. That translates into grades that are short and/or gentle.

This is definitely a good family hike and definitely the easiest way to get to the saddle below Sherman Peak. Although the FS#12 connector (part of hike 31) is a shorter route to the saddle, it's decidedly uphill. For families with two adults, I'd suggest walking in along this trail, downhill back to the Motorway via the connector FS#12, then having one adult walk back down the road for 0.7 miles to retrieve the car.

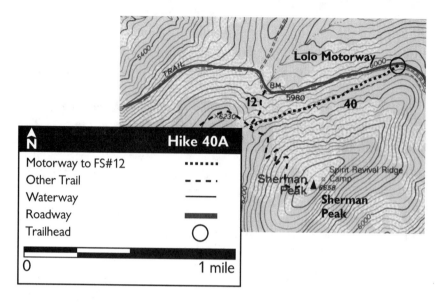

Though short, this hike provides a good variety of plants and scenery, and a close-up look at some standard Motorway trees and understory plants. There are mountain hemlock, subalpine fir, grand fir, lodgepole pine, huckleberry, whortleberry, beargrass, and spirea added in. There are some nice rock outcrops on the uphill side; a couple of nice stream crossings, one with mossy rocks; upstream waterfalls; flowers; and bushes.

In the open spots, there are views into the North Fork of the Clearwater area. Massive, rocky Pot Mountain is the easiest to identify, and to its west there are ridges, almost ad infinitum, in fading colors. Cook Mountain and the pinkish Moose Creek Buttes are to its right and Liz Butte is to its left, the large green lump that is nearest the trail you are on. The ridge leading to Liz Butte originates about 1 mile down the Motorway from this trailhead. Rocky Ridge is visible through the trees, a good example of what I call the "standard Motorway ridge," with Weitas Butte in front of it, treed with lookout, a bit of the rocky top of Little Weitas Butte in front of that. Bald Mountain is visible, too, but more easily seen walking west to east.

Connections: The trail connects with the one to Sherman Peak and with FS#12 (hike 31) back to the Motorway.

B. From FS#12 to Sherman Saddle

Why: Good views of the Selway Crags, Sherman Peak, and Willow Ridge.

Ease: Moderate, 1,600-foot elevation change in 2½ miles.

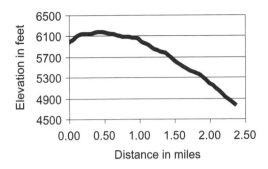

Season: Mid-July through late September.

Maps: CWNF Visitor Map; USGS Liz Butte, Idaho.

Information: Lochsa Ranger District, CWNF, 208-926-4274.

Trailheads: There are two ways to access the east trailhead. Hike FS trail #40/25 (hike 40A), which is on the left at mile 50.4 on the Motorway, for one level mile. Alternatively, take FS#12 (hike 31), which is on the left at mile 51.0 on the Motorway. Both junction with this trail and the one up Sherman Peak at the saddle west of the peak. (Note: There was not yet a

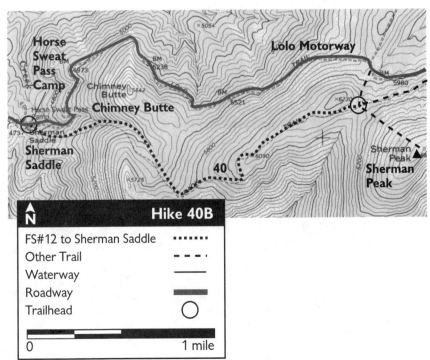

sign at the junction in 2001. The trail from the east joins FS#12 a few yards before this trail separates from the one up Sherman Peak and heads west.

The west trailhead is at Sherman Saddle, mile 53.5 on the Motorway.

The Hike: This is one of those trails where the USGS map really does show just what the hike will be like, though it's the red Lewis and Clark Trail that is an accurate representation on the map, not the black Forest Service Trail. There is a short uphill at the start, then it is downhill the rest of the way. First along the point of the ridge, then turning right to head alongside a pleasant stream before the final downhill stretch to Sherman Saddle. The grade varies from gentle to steep along the way, and there are switchbacks near the western end but not for much of the rest of the trail. The only odd bit is a hard right turn about 1 mile from the west end, but it's obvious and would be difficult to miss.

The trail starts by heading west from its junction with the access trails and the trail up Sherman Peak. Two of the views come early. Turn around before traveling too far, for the excellent and close view of Sherman Peak. A bit later, but while still in the first mile or so of trail, check any openings between the trees on the left for views of the Selway Crags. This trail is

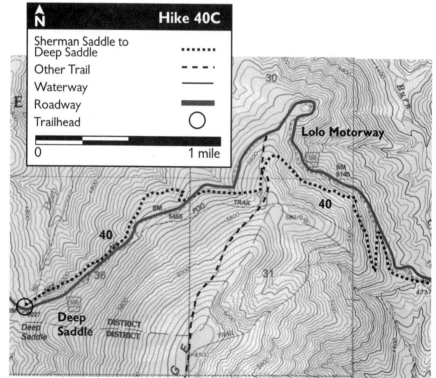

about as close to them as any along the Motorway, 15 miles or so as the crow flies.

Essentially all of the hike is through the woods. Some of the trees are average in size, others are fairly large, 3 feet in diameter or more. The understory is characteristic of most Motorway trails, primarily huckleberry, beargrass, and whortleberry. Sometimes the taller huckleberry bushes dominate, sometimes the shorter plants do.

The trail along the point of the ridge is a bit difficult to follow in places. Although the tread is well-worn and deep, one section was littered with downed lodgepole pines and was hard to follow in 2001. But the trail truly is a deep rut through this area, and there are occasional waterbars across it. Near the point where it turns right and heads toward the creek, there are blazes on the trees, even one that marks the turn. As the trail crosses the small meadows (with blooming flowers in season) at the Sherman Saddle end of the hike, there are close views of Willow Ridge.

Besides history and the views of the Selway Crags, this is a good exercise hike of 2½ miles one-way, especially going west to east for the grade averages 10 percent. But hiking up nearby Willow Ridge (hike 34) for a couple of miles is a better bet as far as views are concerned, especially for views into the North Fork of the Clearwater River, and it too provides a workout.

C. Sherman Saddle to Deep Saddle

Why: Woods, some views.

Ease: Moderate, a long 2½ miles with a 1,000-foot elevation gain up to the Willow Ridge Trail junction, then a 700-foot loss down to Deep Saddle.

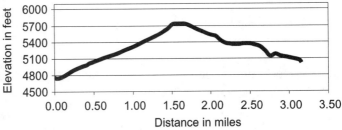

Season: Mid-July through late September.

Maps: CWNF Visitor Map; USGS Liz Butte, Idaho, and Weitas Butte, Idaho. (The USGS topographic maps suggest that more of the trail is above the Motorway than is actually the case.)

Information: Lochsa Ranger District, CWNF, 208-926-4274.

Trailheads: On the left at Sherman Saddle, mile 53.5 on the Motorway. In addition, there are trail signs where the trail crosses the Motorway at miles 53.5 and 55.7.

The Hike: The trail starts to the left of the historic signpost and heads across the meadow. The trailhead sign is a few yards beyond and reads that the trail is both Nee-Me-Poo (FS#40) and Lewis and Clark (FS#25), with Deep Saddle $2\frac{1}{2}$ miles away. I think it's a long $2\frac{1}{2}$ miles.

The first part of the hike is through fine woods of large grand fir and Engelmann spruce. Rock-pile-topped Chimney Butte is visible on occasion, with Sherman Peak above and behind it. Liz Butte and beyond into the North Fork area are visible much of the way. About $\frac{1}{2}$ mile before the trail tops out and intersects with the trail up Willow Ridge (hike 34), there is a glimpse of Pot Mountain. At the trail intersection, the Nee-Me-Poo Trail goes straight ahead, while the Lewis and Clark Trail heads up Willow Ridge.

On the way down to the trail's intersection with the Motorway, $\frac{1}{2}$ mile later, there are brief views of Pot Mountain and Little Weitas Butte, the treed top of Weitas Butte with its lookout peeking over the latter's rocky top. After crossing the Motorway, there is a long 1-mile section down to Deep Saddle. That mile is an exceptionally pleasant woods hike, in and of itself. Along the way there are large Douglas fir and Engelmann spruce, as well as several small and attractive water crossings. Each of the latter is distinct—some with flowers, some with pools and falls, others with ferns and moss-covered rocks.

D. Deep Saddle to Green Saddle
Why: A few views.

Ease: Moderate, about 3 miles one way, with an 800-foot elevation gain, then a 400-foot loss.

Season: Mid-July through late September.

Maps: CWNF Visitor Map; USGS Weitas Butte, Idaho. (The 1994 edition of the latter does not show the part of the trail that is below the Motorway.)

Information: Lochsa Ranger District, CWNF, 208-926-4274.

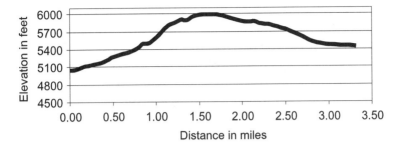

Trailheads: On the right, at the back of the campsite at Deep Saddle, mile 56.8 on the Motorway. There is also a sign where the trail crosses the road at mile 57.6.

The Hike: The first ¾ mile or so of this trail is all uphill, gaining about 300 feet as it passes through woods, crosses a couple of small streams, and, near its west end, works its way through a rock slide. Unfortunately, it also stays fairly close to the Motorway, sometimes just a few feet below it. Through the trees there are occasional limited views toward the North Fork, primarily of Cook and Lookout Mountains.

Most of the rest of the elevation gain for this hike is in the first mile of the trail after it crosses the road. This section moves away from the

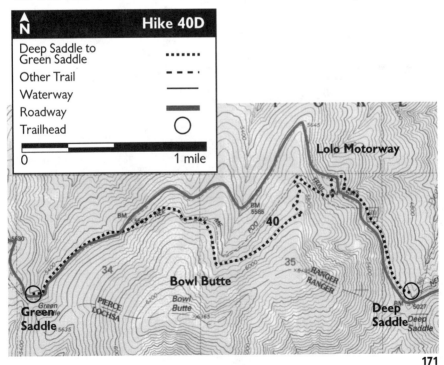

Motorway, circling well below the top of Bowl Butte, and provides a few views through the trees of Cook and Lookout Mountains. From this angle, the former is mostly clear on top, while the latter is more treed and has a flatter slope. Windy Ridge is the bit of land that connects the Motorway to Cook Mountain.

There are switchbacks that cover much of this elevation gain that are not shown on the USGS map. The switchbacks parallel Willow Ridge and provide nice views of the top of Sherman Peak just over the shoulder of Willow Ridge, Bald Mountain, and Castle Butte. Beyond the switchbacks there are two faint forks along this stretch of trail. Take the left in both cases.

If it's a hot day, stop and enjoy the stream about ¹⁄₂ mile before the trail reaches the road. There are pools, moss-covered rocks, yellow violets, white queen cups, and magenta shooting stars. Cool-off spots like this are worth their weight in gold during July. The last ¹⁄₂ mile of this hike is along the road.

> There's an area of bent trees in this section of the hike. More than one person has told me that they heard the Native Americans bent trees as trail markers, and certainly that's where I see these trees—along trails. One person suggested that this explanation might have originated in Boy Scout lore. Others say the trees were bent by heavy winter snow. And another suggested that there have never been enough Native Americans in this area to account for all the bent trees. My only comment is that of course I see these trees along the trails, because that's where I hike.

E. Green Saddle to Weitas Meadows

Why: Nice start and finish.

Ease: Easy, with an approximate 370-foot elevation gain and 360-foot loss over 2 miles.

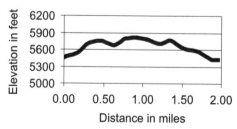

Season: Mid-July through late September.

Maps: CWNF Visitor Map; USGS Weitas Butte, Idaho.

Information: Lochsa Ranger District, CWNF, 208-926-4274.

Trailheads: The east end is on the left at Green Saddle, mile 60.1 on the Motorway. The west end is on the left on the road into Weitas Meadows, which is at mile 62.4 on the Motorway. There also are signs where the trail crosses the Motorway at miles 60.7, 60.9, 61.3, and 61.4.

The Hike:

My favorite parts of this hike are its start and finish. From Green Saddle, the trail is uphill. In early July, it's lined with blooming beargrass that look like lanterns guiding the way out of the saddle and up the hill. On the west end, there's Weitas Meadows. In the early morning light, that means dew on the grasslike sedges that surround the small stream meandering through, and a few clumps of trees. Weitas Meadows doesn't need flowers in bloom to make it a special place.

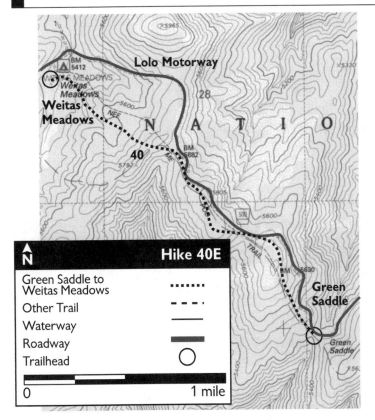

As it lays now, this is an odd hike. It intersects the Motorway twice and runs parallel and within a few feet of it in a third spot. Perhaps its path will be changed if the Beaver Dam Saddle to Weitas Meadows section is reconstructed.

The mileage sign just up the hill from the historic sign post at Green Saddle reads Weitas Meadows, 2 miles, Beaver Dam Saddle, 10 miles. The trail is largely uphill for $3/4$ mile to the first road intersection, where the trail and the road coincide for maybe $1/10$ of a mile. Then there is more up and down to the next road intersection about $1/2$ mile later. At this one, there are only a few yards of Motorway walking required. Then the trail is largely downhill to the meadows.

The trees along the way are fine, Engelmann spruce and mountain hemlock primarily, with the largest trees at the highest elevations. The woods feel pleasantly open and nonconfining.

At the meadow end, the trail becomes a log-lined thoroughfare filled with gravel. Please stay on the thoroughfare. It helps preserve the fragile wet area that the trail passes through. As you walk, do note the lovely meadow.

F. Motorway to Motorway

Why: A short hike.

Ease: Easy, about $1/3$ mile in length.

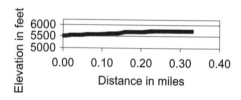

Season: Mid-July through late September.

Maps: CWNF Visitor Map; USGS Weitas Butte, Idaho. (The trail is not on either map.)

Information: Lochsa Ranger District, CWNF, 208-926-4274.

Trailhead: On the right at mile 62.5 on the Motorway. The other end is at mile 62.9.

The Hike: This is a short leg-stretcher through fairly close woods of small-to medium-sized trees and average-sized understory. It heads uphill and intersects with the Motorway about $1/4 - 3/8$ mile from its start. The uphill is steepest at first, becomes more gentle, and eventually levels off. There are no views along the way.

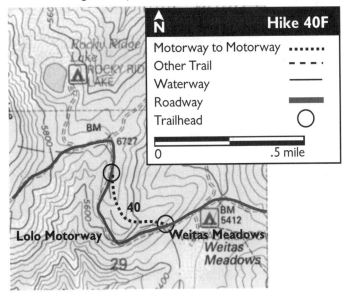

G. Rocky Ridge Overview to Motorway

Why: A very short leg-stretcher.

Ease: Easy, about $1/10$ mile in length.

Season: Mid-July through late September.

Maps: CWNF Visitor Map; USGS Weitas Butte, Idaho. (The trail is not on either map.)

Information: Lochsa Ranger District, CWNF, 208-926-4274.

Trailhead: On the right at mile 63.8 on the Motorway. The other end is at mile 63.9.

The Hike: This extremely short trail segment starts to the left of the Rocky Ridge Overview sign and heads slightly back into the woods for a brief way before returning to the Motorway.

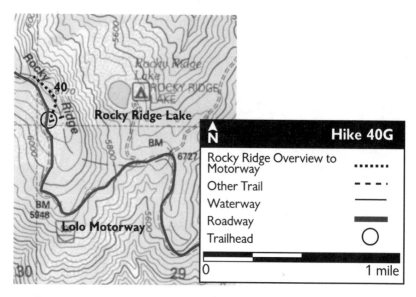

H. Motorway to Beaver Dam Saddle

Why: Fine woods.

Ease: Easy to moderate, about 1 mile in length with an approximate 600-foot elevation change.

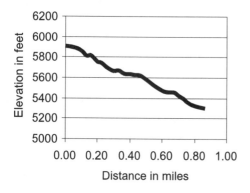

Season: Mid-July through late September.

Maps: CWNF Visitor Map; USGS Snowy Summit, Idaho. (However, the trail is not on the 1984 photorevised edition of the latter.)

Information: Lochsa Ranger District, CWNF, 208-926-4274.

Trailhead: The trailhead is on the right at mile 67.0 on the Motorway.

The Hike: The mileage sign a few yards beyond the trailhead reads ¾ mile to Beaver Dam Saddle. I think it's a long ¾ mile, though it may feel shorter because the entire hike is well graded and downhill. Even if it's hiked in the reverse direction, the going never gets really tough—it's obviously uphill, but that's about as bad as it gets.

Right at the start of the hike there are some quick views of Pot Mountain and of the ridges of the Mallard-Larkins area to the northwest of it. The Mallard-Larkins is a series of gentle ridges and peaks, a roadless area with high alpine lakes and extraordinarily friendly mountain goats.

From then on, it is a shaded walk in the woods, primarily tall and large mountain hemlock and Engelmann spruce. The understory is bright green, a pleasant contrast to the trees' bark: slabby and dark for the mountain hemlock, scaly and dark for the spruce. About ¼ mile in, the sign for water points down to a trickle below the trail.

There is a trail reroute near the end of the hike that may or may not be visible in years to come. It provides clues for deciding whether any section of Forest Service designated historic trail is on or close to the actual tread or whether it has been rerouted at some point during the past—whether it is ancient Nez Perce or the 1866 trail route, for example. At this point, there has been a reroute because the obliterated trail is on the ridgeline, as would be expected for ancient Nez Perce trail, while the rerouted trail is not.

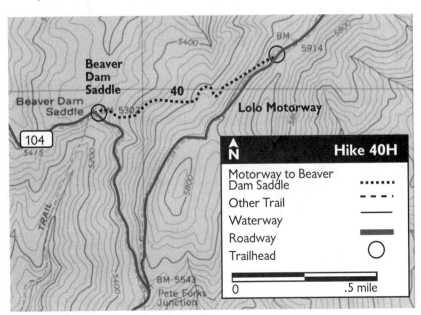

177

I. Beaver Dam Saddle to Camp Martin

Why: Fine hemlock woods.

Ease: Moderate to strenuous, with an approximate 800-foot of elevation gain and a 900-foot loss over 5 miles.

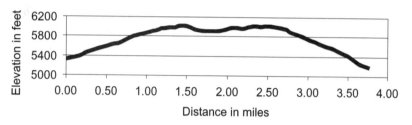

Season: Mid-July through late September.

Maps: CWNF Visitor Map; USGS Snowy Summit, Idaho.

Information: Lochsa Ranger District, CWNF, 208-926-4274.

Trailheads: Turn on to the road to Beaver Dam Saddle at mile 68.0 on the Motorway and drive 0.7 miles to the trailhead. The Camp Martin trailhead is 5.0 miles farther along the same 104 Road.

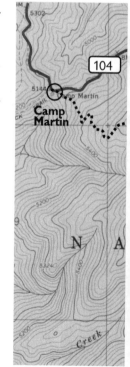

The Hike: Beaver Dam Saddle was formerly known as Pond Saddle because of the small ponds that were located there. The ponds are silted in now, probably due to erosion that resulted from fires that burned in the area between 1866 and the 1930s.

There are three segments to this section of trail, all separated by road crossings. The first contains the finest of the hemlock woods, the second is difficult to follow, and the third has fine woods and a brief look at Pot Mountain on the North Fork of the Clearwater River. In many places in all of the sections there are signs of trail rerouting, but the old trails are camouflaged with branches and the like.

The trail heads out of Beaver Dam Saddle, between

the roads and just to the right of the road sign. A few feet up the hill, a sign reads Camp Martin 5 miles, Lolo Forks 11, and Musselshell Meadows 16.

The trail continues uphill with the road visible on the left for a few yards, but in less than a mile it is in a forest made up primarily of two-plus foot in diameter hemlock trees. It is dark and shady, at least early in the day, in places almost as dark as a cedar forest. But not quite, for there is a bit of understory here as opposed to a cedar woods, where there is often none.

This part of the hike feels much like a walk in the park except for one confusing bit. The trail is indistinct as it travels the edge of a rocky area about 1 mile into the hike. I suggest leaving a marker as you exit the woods and enter the rocky area, for the connection seems harder on the way back down. On the way up, keep to the left to find the trail. On the way down, turn right when entering the rocky area and walk along the definite groove that heads down the slope. There is a blaze and a Nee-Me-Poo metal trail marker on a tree on the left soon after it becomes more obvious that this is the trail.

The first road crossing is after a couple of miles. Turn to the right and walk about 0.2 mile to where the trail takes off to the left for its second segment. It is signed at that point.

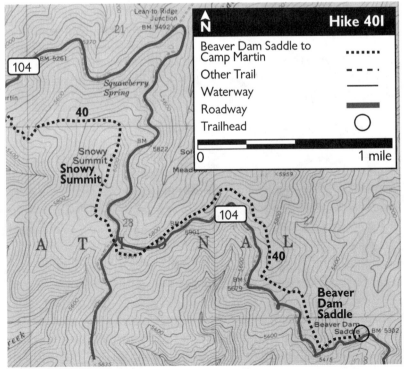

The second segment is difficult to follow in places until the trail reaches the top. Basically, it stays just to the right of the center and highest area. After it tops out, the trail heads down to cross the second road, signed to Snowy Summit but actually heading to the old lookout site. (An easy alternative to hiking the second segment is to avoid it entirely by staying on the main road for 0.4 mile, until it intersects with that road signed to Snowy Summit.)

Go straight across the road and between the small hemlocks. (In 2001, the trail sign was face down on the ground under the fallen tree that held it.) Guide to the left along the trail, then follow the same general trajectory through some downed trees, then a bit more to the right through a small opening. The trail then switchbacks up to a more open area with large hemlock, then other trees. It skirts Snowy Summit and ends in a woods of small lodgepole, heading down 800 feet along decently graded switchbacks to Camp Martin. There are a few views of Hemlock Ridge and its lookout, of prairie, and of Pot Mountain.

Note: Hiking from Camp Martin, the trail is shorter. Or that's what the sign at that end suggests: Beaver Dam Saddle 4 miles.

J. Camp Martin to Lolo Forks

Why: Outstanding big trees between Camp Martin and above Lolo Forks.

Ease: Moderate hiking east to west, strenuous hiking west to east. There is a 2,700-foot elevation change over about 6 miles of trail, plus a few more feet from working across the various saddles.

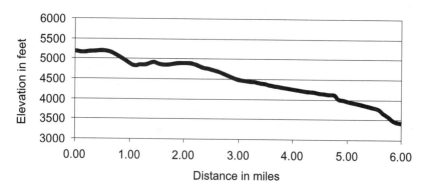

Season: Early June through October from Lolo Forks. The road to Camp Martin may not be available until early July when the Motorway is open.

Maps: CWNF Visitor Map; USGS Hemlock Butte, Idaho, and Snowy Summit, Idaho.

Information: Lochsa Ranger District, CWNF, 208-926-4274.

Trailheads: The trailhead at Camp Martin is 5.7 miles up the 104 Road, which turns off the Motorway at mile 68.0, Pete Forks Junction. (The 104 Road is part of the original Lolo Motorway.) The trail starts to the right of the Camp Martin sign as an overgrown road but rapidly transforms into a trail.

Alternately, to reach the lower trailhead and hike up, turn off Highway 12 on to Woodland Road at the bridge over the Clearwater River in Kamiah. In 0.4 mile, turn right at the Forest Access sign. Stay right 1.6 miles later. The road surface changes to gravel 10 miles farther (unless it has since been paved by the county), then becomes paved again in 6 miles at the Y in the road. Stay to the left at the Y. The Lolo Campground is 6.2 miles farther. Stay left on the 100 Road shortly after the campground, then turn right on the 103 Road in 4.8 miles. Cross Yoosa Creek in 4.6 miles. The Lolo Forks trailhead is on the left immediately after the creek.

The Hike: The original trail from Camp Martin to Lolo Forks was that of the Northern Nez Perce. The lower portion was rerouted when the current trail was first constructed in 1866 by the Bird-Truax Expedition, who also named Lolo Forks. Later, when the Forest Service established a ranger station at Musselshell Meadows, it began building a network of trails to the northeast, east, and southeast. Since this segment of the Bird-Truax Trail was still in use and located where they wanted a trail, it was cleaned out and became part of the network.

Hunters kept the trail cleared when it fell into disuse after the Lolo Motorway was constructed in the early 1930s, and the trail also was cleared in the 1980s for the Appaloosa Horse Club ride up the ridge. The last changes came in the 1990s, when the Forest Service rehabilitated the lower part and tried to keep the route historically accurate. At that time, they built the new packbridge over Lolo Creek.

Timber has been harvested in the lower portion of the trail, and there have been intense fires on the upper part. But in the middle, there are huge old-growth trees.

Camp Martin was named after fur trapper D. W. Martin who lived at Musselshell Meadows in the early 1900s.

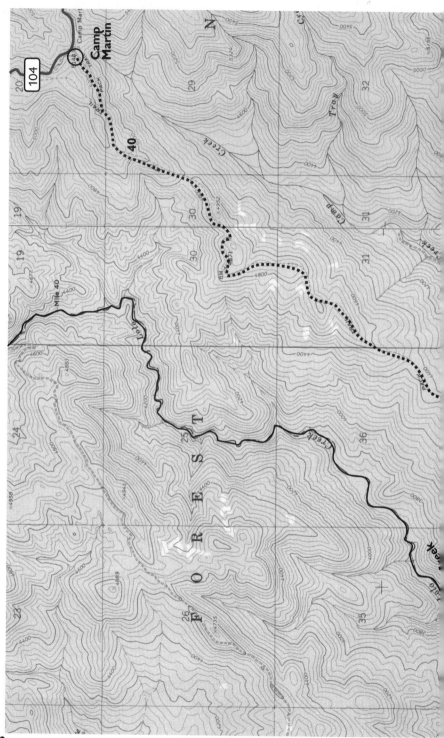

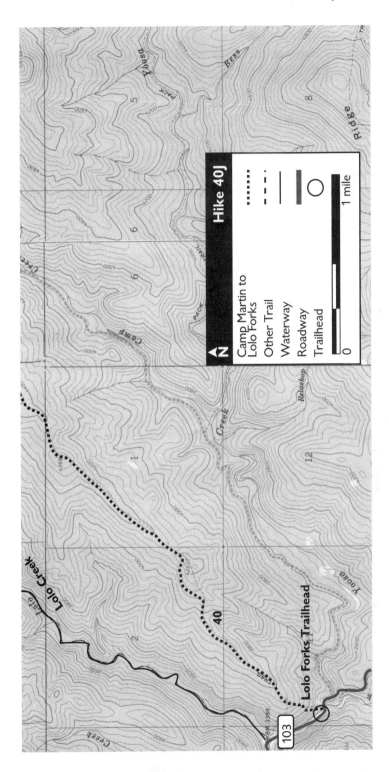

Hike 40J

Camp Martin to Lolo Forks

····· Other Trail
---- Trail
▬▬ Waterway
Roadway
○ Trailhead

0 _____ 1 mile

N

The area is home to the black bear. Steve encountered one during midafternoon of a hot sunny day. The bear and he met in a clear-cut area on the lower portion of the trail. The sighting was simultaneous, and the bear crashed off into the brush a few yards and waited for Steve to pass.

If hiking from the top down and then back up, this is one hike where stopping short of the trail's end makes sense. The bottom 2 miles of this trail aren't pretty, and in spots, they're not in good condition either. But the top 4 miles are a delight.

The trail from Camp Martin is level for about $1/4$ mile and contains skunky, overgrown bits like those at the Lolo Forks end. Then it heads more steeply downhill for about a mile before attaining the gentler grade it holds throughout the rest of the hike. It loosely follows the ridgeline, moving from open areas to woods to the edges of woods, and moving across saddles to follow the right or left side of the ridge. There are occasional views out toward Kamiah and the prairie south of it, to Snowy Summit, and the parallel section of the Lolo Divide to the southeast.

But the views aren't the reason to hike this trail, the trees are. There are larch, grand fir, Engelmann spruce, Douglas fir, ponderosa pine, white pine, and cedar, to name just the big ones. And they are big. In most places, most of them are more than two-and-one-half feet in diameter. In mid-hike, there are places where all are at least three to four feet wide. Big trees.

The mix of species varies from place to place, sometimes including Pacific yew, and at the lower elevations there are areas where essentially all are cedar, with little or no ground cover beneath.

The last couple of miles down feature poor trail that is often out in the open and often overgrown—a huge contrast to the just-hiked $3 1/2$ miles of excellent, sometimes needle-soft, trail. The trail crosses a road about $1/2$ mile from the bottom, at which point, turn right and walk about 20 paces to find the bottom section. The trail then junctions with the connector trail up from Lolo Forks. Turn left to reach the road, or go right to hike on toward Musselshell Meadows.

There are two spots where it is a bit difficult to keep to the trail, especially if hiking uphill. The first is about 4 miles up and is the result of a salt lick not far from the end of an open area, a place where one of the many intersecting game trails along the route can fool a hiker. The trail is in the open with many overhanging snowbushes. It actually veers to the left, but that is not apparent because of the heavily used, straight-ahead game route to the salt lick. If you end up at the salt lick, either backtrack to find where the trail ducks into and under a snowbush and the trees, or just make a 90-degree left and walk into the trees until you find the trail.

The second is $1/2$ mile or so later, at an open saddle with several downed trees that hide the trail. Heading uphill, head to the left side of the ridge.

When the trail is in the trees, it is blazed and keeping to it is not a problem.

K. Lolo Forks to Musselshell Meadows

Why: Nice trees and a quiet picnic spot on Siberia Creek.

Ease: Moderate, with a 500-foot elevation gain and 700-foot loss over 5 miles.

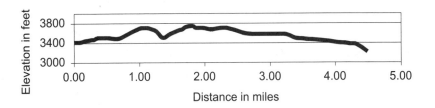

Season: May through late October.

Maps: CWNF Visitor Map; USGS Hemlock Butte, Idaho, and Musselshell, Idaho.

Information: Lochsa Ranger District, CWNF, 208-926-4274.

Trailheads: Turn off Highway 12 on to Woodland Road at the bridge over the Clearwater River in Kamiah. In 0.4 mile, turn right at the Forest Access sign. Stay right 1.6 miles later. The road surface changes to gravel 10 miles farther (unless it has since been paved by the county), then becomes paved again 6 miles later at the Y in the road. Stay to the left at the Y. The Lolo Campground is 6.2 miles farther. Stay left on the 100 Road shortly after the campground, then turn right on the 103 Road in 4.8 miles. Cross Yosha Creek in 4.6 miles. The Lolo Forks trailhead is on the left immediately after the creek.

Alternately, to find the Musselshell Meadows trailhead from Weippe, head straight east out of town on Pierce Road. At Peterson Corners, where the main road makes a sharp left turn, continue straight at mile marker 8 on the 100 Road, then continue for an additional 3.6 miles and turn left at Musselshell Meadows.

The Musselshell Meadows trailhead is on the right, 1 mile up the 535 Road after its junction with the 100 Road.

The Hike: The trail to Musselshell from Lolo Forks begins on the left fork at the end of the short connector trail up from the 103 Road. It quickly crosses the creek and a small meadow before heading into the woods to the right of a large cedar—one of several large trees along this trail. The trail briefly stays by the creek, then heads uphill and into more woods as it traces the contours of the hillsides above Lolo Creek. The understory is short and visibility is good, but there are no views along the way.

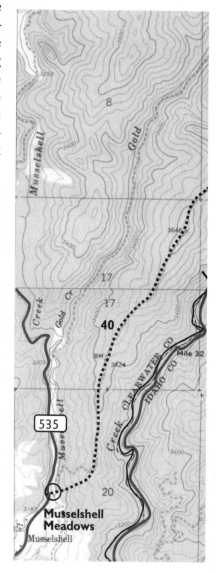

At Siberia Creek, about $1^3/_4$ miles into the hike, there is a tree that has fallen across the creek and obscured the trail. It also is the tree that has the trail sign on it.

The Siberia Creek area is worth some time and is a choice picnic spot. The bright green understory is highlighted by dappled sunlight and is a fine contrast to the gray cedar trunks. There are a few Pacific yew and small maples, and the creek is small and quiet.

Once across the creek, the trail heads primarily uphill until it merges left on to an old road that was part of the original Lolo Motorway. A sign at this junction indicates that it is 2 miles from Lolo Forks and 3 miles to Musselshell Meadows.

Over the first mile or so after this

sign, several roads intersect the old road the trail is on. Stay to the right at each. Soon after that mile, the trail will become just a trail again when it swings left off the road and into the woods. While there was no sign at this junction in 2000, the road straight ahead was partially blocked by downed trees. From the junction, it is about another mile to the trail sign at the Meadows.

Note: Musselshell Meadows became the primary camas-gathering ground for the Nez Perce after the Weippe Prairie was settled by whites.

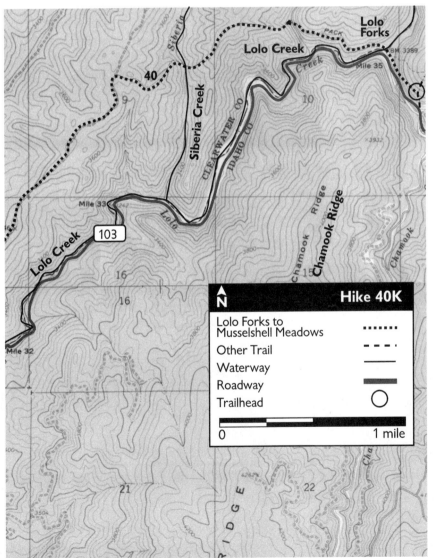

A Nez Perce legend tells the origin of the Nee-Me-Poo Trail. A young boy was lost in these mountains. He was approached by Hah-hahts, the grizzly bear, who was angry that the humans were taking over his land. When confronted, the boy said, "I can only die. Death is only a part of life. I am not afraid." The grizzly, impressed with his bravery, took the boy to the "backbone of the highest mountains" to show him where the quas-peet-za, the curled hairs, lived. He also showed him the huckleberry, chokecherry, and serviceberry. When they returned to the Kamiah Valley, before leaving him, the bear said, "Here your people are living. Go tell them what you have learned about this great land, the food that has been provided for them, and the trail that will take them across the mountains." (*This legend was told to Sandi McFarland by her relatives and passed along to me by her.*)

There are three trails at Howard Creek. One goes east, one goes west, and one is a small loop designed to illustrate the differences between modern and ancient trails.

Why: Easy access from Highway 12 to sections of historic trail traveled by the Nee-Me-Poo, Lewis and Clark, and many others. Walking them will leave you with a renewed respect for all who have walked them before you.

Ease: Easy to moderate, given that in places they are steep, narrow, and slant to the outside. The east and west trails may not be suitable for small children due to the occasional narrowness of trail and steep sidehills, especially on the west section.

Season: The trails are open year-round, but you can expect them to have snow in the winter.

Maps: LNF Visitor Map; USGS Garden Point, Montana.

Information: Missoula Ranger District, LNF, 406-329-3814.

Trailheads: Howard Creek is at milepost 14 on Highway 12 in Montana. The east trailhead is a few yards up the road behind the large trail information sign, just before the sign for the 238 Road. There is a tree with a historical trail marker just down the trail from the start. The trailhead for the west segment and the loop is on the left, across the forest service road from the information sign.

The trails at Howard Creek were used for hundreds of years, both by the Nez Perce heading for central Montana to hunt buffalo, and by the Salish heading west from Montana to fish for salmon on the upper Lochsa River. Lewis and Clark walked this tread in September 1805, and again the following June.

Use of the trail decreased when the Lolo Hot Springs became more of a tourist destination in the late 1800s, which is when the wagon road up Lolo

Creek was extended to accommodate the increased tourist traffic to the springs.

The Bird-Truax Expedition passed over this section of trail several times. Because their wagon road was never built, and because improvements to their trail were made from the western end and stopped short of Lolo Pass, this segment of trail was not rerouted by them.

This trail segment is part of the historic Nee-Me-Poo Trail and was traveled by the Nez Perce in 1877 as they fled Idaho.

The tread does not seem as deeply eroded as one might expect from a trail so long and heavily used. This is because trails change over time, even when they are not used. Shrubs and trees can grow in an unused trail, and they trap soil. Fire may open hillsides to erosion, which may fill or completely erase trail tread. Wild game and gravity work to reduce the outer edge or shoulder of the tread, and that works to at least visually reduce the depth of the trail.

The Hikes

Hike 41. The Trail East: The start of the trail heading east might make it look as though the old trails weren't so bad, just a bit narrow. But only at the start. Within a few hundred yards, it shoots what feels like straight up the hillside at a 30% grade for 100 feet or so. From then on, it's not a distant scenery hike. It's a hike where it's important to watch the narrow trail and where you put your feet, even when it's not steep. It's a trail where the immediate surroundings are what will be seen. Fortunately, the rocks along it are varied, and, at least in mid-May, there is a nice selection of flowers.

The trail intersects with a grown-over road after a mile. Head down the road a few paces, and look for the trail sign on a big larch to the left. The trail

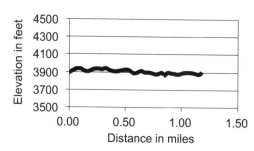

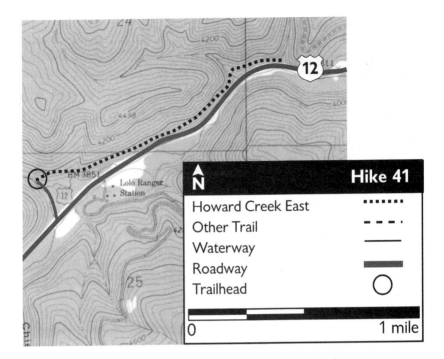

Hike 41	
Howard Creek East	....
Other Trail	- - - - '
Waterway	————
Roadway	▬▬
Trailhead	○
0	1 mile

then continues for a short distance farther.

There were both Lewis and Clark and Nee-Me-Poo signs at the trail's end in 2001, which was a bit more than a mile from the trailhead.

Hike 42. The Comparison Loop: This loop illustrates three ways to distinguish between true historical and reconstructed trails: the pitch, the length of switchbacks, and width.

The loop starts with a couple of switchbacks on a wide, well-graded path through the trees. There are spruce, fir, and larch, and in mid-May, trillium underneath. The transition to historic trail after a few hundred yards is abrupt, at a sign reading, "Original Lolo Trail, Use Caution—Steep Trail. Parking Lot Left, Howard Creek West to the Right."

Turn left to complete the loop on what is the widest bit of historical trail in the area, and the least steep. (The second few hundred yards of the Howard Creek East Trail is a better illustration of steep.) There is even a shallow switchback on the way down to the parking lot. The trail ends a few yards closer to the highway than it began.

Hike 43. The Trail West: The trail west begins along the section of new trail shared with the loop, a couple of gentle switchbacks through the woods before the historically accurate section. The trail then traces the contours of the occasionally steep hillside it travels and passes above some fine rock outcrops, staying in the woods for about a half mile, then passing through an open hillside, and on through an area logged about 1990. The logging left tall trees dotting the hillside, primarily ponderosa pine, and did not disturb the trail tread. There are occasional historic trail signs along the way, triangles on the trees with Nee-Me-Poo on one side of the tree and Lewis and Clark on the other.

The trail ends at a saddle with a road intersection. There is no indication that it continues beyond that point. At the saddle, there is a quick peek at Lolo Peak and of nearby hillsides on the south side of the road and creek.

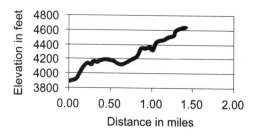

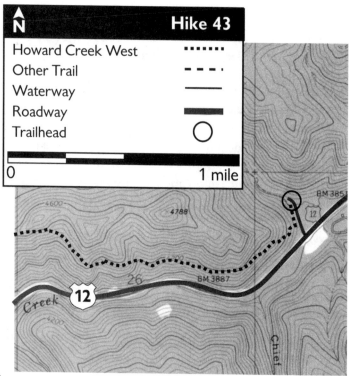

The latter show a fair bit of human usage. In early July, there was an abundance of allium, a wild onion, in bloom, and of spotted knapweed, an invasive species.

Except for a small segment of the loop trail, all these trails are managed as historical trails, which means they are approximately in the same condition as they were when they were walked hundreds of years ago.

Note: More miles of this trail may be available for hiking in the future.

Why: An easy, informative hike through woods and cut-over areas.

Ease: Easy, with gentle grades over $2\frac{1}{2}$ miles of trail.

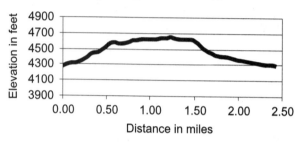

Season: The trail can be hiked year-round, but expect snow in the winter. If the campground is closed, park at the gate and walk back to the trailhead.

Maps: LNF Visitor Map; USGS Lolo Hot Springs, Montana.

Information: Missoula Ranger District, LNF, 406-329-3814.

Trailhead: On the left at the Lee Creek Campground, mileposts 5–6 on Highway 12 in Montana. The trailhead is on the left at the head of the road into the campground loop. Trail guides are available there.

The Hike: Pick up a trail guide before heading out on this trail. It explains what is illustrated at each numbered stop along the trail and has a four-species evergreen tree identifier.

The trail has two sections. The first is about 2 miles long and through woods of varying ages and stages. The second is a $\frac{1}{2}$ mile return to the trailhead along a Forest Service road.

The trail starts with a gentle uphill, a reminder that even easy trails will have ups and downs. It is no problem to follow and is a fine place to see large trees and to examine different forests: old ones, young ones, and cut-over ones. It is also a good place to learn to distinguish between the bark of ponderosa pine and that of mature larch. The two species occur almost side by side in many spots, as seed trees left after a timber harvest in one area and in the woods in many others. Superficially, their bark is quite similar, orangish and rough. Ponderosa pine bark, however, looks cracked and appears to be made from jigsaw puzzle pieces. Larch bark just looks rough. There also are large Douglas fir along the trail. Their bark is intensely layered and usually has some orange color at the base of deep grooves.

Connections: The trail intersects with two other trails within a short distance of the start. Go straight at both intersections. Near the junction of the trail and the road at the end of the hike, the trail intersects with FS#295. Turn right to reach the road in 1/4 mile and the campground in 3/4 mile. Alternatively, turn around and walk back to the campground through the woods, for the walk along the road isn't very interesting, though it is much shorter.

At the point the trail reaches the road, there is a sign for the Lee Ridge Trail #295. You can walk the interpretive trail in the opposite direction by entering here, but there are no trail guides at that point.

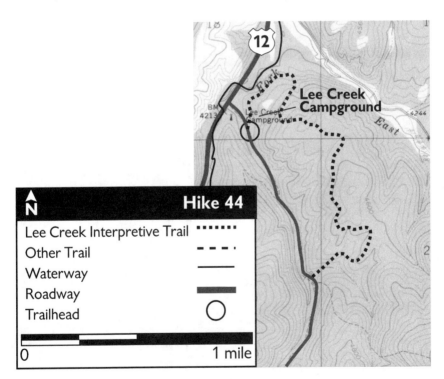

Appendixes

Additional Hikes

There are two types of hikes included here. The first are trails I've hiked that I don't recommend unless you have lots of time. Other, similar, hikes are better in my opinion. The second type are trails I haven't hiked but have included so that if you see the trailhead signs, you'll know something about the trail. One of these, from Powell to Wendover off Highway 12, is of special interest due to its historical significance. Most of both types are signed and maintained by the Forest Service.

Off Highway 12:

■ Brushy Fork, FS#34, off forest road 369 between Powell and Lolo Pass. Although this trail is still on the CWNF Visitor maps, when checked in 2000 it was almost impossible to find the trailhead and essentially impossible to hike the trail.

■ Lewis and Clark Trail #25 from Wendover to Powell. This trail follows the route of the Corps of Discovery on September 15, 1805, when they left their camp near today's Powell and climbed up Wendover Ridge to camp at Snowbank Camp. The first section of trail, about 1½ miles from Wendover around behind Whitehorse Pond to the Papoose Creek Road, is finished and is a relatively level hike along this historic route. But lack of access to private property between there and Powell meant, in 2001, that the trail was not completed and that it was not possible to hike from that road to Powell. (The trail also goes along the creek from White Sands Campground through the Powell Ranger District to Powell Campground.) Check with the Forest Service for up-to-date information. Note: Powell was named for Charley Powell, a trapper who built a cabin there about 1903.

■ Mocus Point, FS#469, milepost 143. Another uphill hike with few views except for glimpses up and down the Lochsa. If you want to hike uphill on this side of the Lochsa, hike Lochsa Peak, hike 11. It is a harder hike, but there are good views.

■ Weir Creek Hot Springs, mileposts 142–143. I've not hiked this user-maintained trail but am told it's about a mile to the springs.

■ Eagle Mountain, FS#206, mileposts 135–136. Same comment as Mocus Point.

■ Holly Creek, FS#122, mileposts 131–132. This trail is maintained but not yet signed and starts just a few feet downriver from the creek crossing itself. It's steeply uphill, 1 1/2 miles long, and even in July of a low-water year, the creek crossings result in wet socks. There are no views.

Split Creek, FS#133, mileposts 111–112. I've not hiked this trail because I've heard not one good thing about it. It's out in the open, heavily uphill, and after 8 miles you can still hear the traffic on Highway 12. It does take you to the Chimney Peak area and is probably okay if you have horses.

Van Camp, FS#16, mileposts 107–108. Heavily used by off-highway vehicles and bikes.

Deadman Ridge, FS#142, milepost 105. This is an uphill hike with few views in the first couple of miles. If you want to be uphill on this side of the Lochsa, hike Fish Butte, hike 14. You'll see views within 2 miles.

Glade Creek, FS#111, mileposts 104–105, is not signed and maintained. It's hikeable and easy to follow for at least 2 miles, but it's uphill after the first 1/4 mile, with no views to speak of.

The Lee Creek Trails out of the Lee Creek Campground in Montana, mileposts 6–7 on Highway 12. Neither offers any scenery and, in fact, both head through recently cut-over areas. The westernmost of the trails is not easy to follow in places. Both are fine as cross-country ski trails when the area is blanketed in many feet of snow.

Off the Motorway:

Weitas Creek, FS#174, from 12-Mile Saddle at mile 38.4. This trail is open to four-wheel off-road vehicles for 8 miles from this trailhead. Although it is worth hiking for the meadows along the creek about 2–4 miles in, and the grade is gentle, the fact that it's an ORV trail puts it into the appendix.

Gass Creek, FS#254, at mile 65.5. It heads downhill and offers almost no views. For views, try Willow Ridge, No-see-um Butte, or the short trails to various old lookout sites. The creek is named for Sergeant Gass of the Corps of Discovery.

Flame Ridge, FS#123, 3.2 miles up the road to the Weitas Butte lookout. The trail heads down the ridge into an old cedar grove that was untouched by the fires of the early 1900s. It is pleasant walking, but the trail becomes difficult to find after about 1 1/2 miles. If maintained, it's done by outfitters.

Fish Creek Meadows, FS#230, 1.2 miles down the road to Boundary Peak. The trail has some lovely large trees and heads down to Fish Creek, however, it is rarely, if ever, maintained and becomes difficult to follow due to downed trees and general lack of use.

■ Austin Ridge to Eldorado Creek, FS#48 and FS#31. The Austin Ridge Trail is off the Motorway, and the Eldorado Creek Trail is off the 524 Road. The ridge trail is steep in places and offers no views. The intersecting trail up Eldorado Creek is fine for the first couple of miles, then not maintained and hard to find. (I'm told there's a grove of huge cedars along this creek, but they must be beyond the part of the trail that is maintained.) You can hike the FS#32 trail, which takes off from the FS#31 trail and also intersects with the FS#48 trail.

Eldorado Creek was called Fish Creek by Lewis and Clark, for the large fish they saw there. Miners gave it the current name, after a place of great riches in mining lore.

Off the Selway River:

■ Rackliff, FS#702, 7.8 miles off Highway 12 on the Selway River Road. A very uphill hike, 5,100 feet in total up to the ridgetop. In the first few miles, the views are only of Coolwater Ridge. Hiking uphill off the Selway is best done on the Glover Ridge Trail, hike 18.

■ East Boyd, FS#703, 10.5 miles off Highway 12 on the Selway River Road. Same comments as Rackliff, though this is only 4,800 feet to the ridgetop.

The Motorway is a rugged, narrow, often dusty, one-lane dirt road with numerous sharp rocks and boulders, holes, and other obstructions. It is not certain at the time of this writing whether standard sedan-type vehicles will be allowed to drive it. Even if they are allowed, we strongly urge that you not drive the Motorway with anything that does not have pick-up-truck clearance. Good tires are a must, as is a full-sized spare tire.

Parking and camping areas—the latter all primitive—are limited along the Motorway. There is no potable water. Each vehicle must contain a shovel and a pail. The shovel and pail are required by Idaho state law for travel off main roads during the fire season, and if the Motorway is open for travel, it is the fire season.

Note: During and around the years of the bicentennial of the Lewis and Clark Expedition, access to most of the Motorway may be limited to those with permits, and camping spaces may be assigned. (See resource section for information.)

Most, if not all, of the information necessary for hiking the trails is contained within this book. There are directions to the trailhead, hike descriptions, maps, elevation profiles, and sometimes suggestions as to whether individual hikes can be shortened or lengthened to fit individual needs. Information on side trails or other features of note are included.

Full-sized, 1:24,000 USGS maps are not included in this book, nor are they available anywhere along the highway between Missoula, Montana, and Lewiston or Moscow, Idaho, or Spokane, Washington. (USGS maps for the CWNF are available only at the Forest Service's main office in Orofino, Idaho.)

The trail maps are as usable and accurate as we can make them. Mary has hiked every inch of trail included in the book except for a $^3/_4$ mile stretch of the No-see-um Butte Trail, which means the hiking descriptions are written from the personal experience of just one person and should be fairly consistent.

Be sure to check with the appropriate Forest Service office to determine whether anything has happened that affects trails you are interested in hiking. They can provide up-to-date information on trails and roads and will know if trailhead passes of any kind are required. As of this writing, passes are not required in Idaho or Montana.

That information is not only handy but also essential. Trails can be relocated, poorly maintained, or closed due to animal problems. Trailheads can be moved. Trail numbers can be changed. Roads can be washed out, closed, or relocated. And there can be changes to trails and roads due to logging or fire. There were many of the latter circumstances during the summer of 2000, when most of the trails in the book were hiked.

Check on local hunting seasons. They usually are not a problem here, especially for day hikers. But it is wise to avoid the first week or so of elk season anywhere and to wear blaze orange from then on. Note: There are spring turkey- and bear-hunting seasons.

If you are still at home when reading this book and planning your hike(s), call the appropriate Forest Service office for up-to-date information. It saves disappointment at best, serious problems at worst. It also would be wise to order both USGS and Forest Service Visitor maps. (See the resource section.)

If you are already en route, stop at a Forest Service office for Forest Service Visitor maps and to ask for information. Check out the weather forecast, too, especially early and late in the season.

Keep in mind that the hiking for this book was done in 2000 and 2001. Things will have changed since then.

Most of these suggestions are simply common sense, but all are worth noting and keeping in mind.

....

Stay on the trail.

Don't hike alone.

Don't hike at night.

Don't split up your group.

Let the slowest hiker set the pace.

Especially early in the season, pace yourself to avoid becoming overtired.

Regularly check where you are on the USGS maps.

Don't drink the water unless it's been boiled, filtered, or treated. See the notes on purification in the Dangers section of this book.

Don't eat anything wild unless you can absolutely and positively identify it as edible.

Keep your eyes open—for signs of animals and on the weather, especially early and late in the season but also in high elevations.

Carry a walking or trekking stick. They have several uses, for example, as a third leg for balance or for defense.

Be careful crossing streams.

Don't swim lakes or streams.

Don't slide down snowy fields or rocky slopes.

Do think ahead. Consider the hazards that might be met along the trail and review ahead of time what to do for each.

What If Something Happens?*

The most important thing to do if something happens is to think. Don't panic. Sit down, take a few deep breaths, take a drink or two of water, and then assess the situation.

Sit down, because if you are not moving, you probably can't make the situation worse.

Take a few deep breaths, because they will help you to calm down and feel in control.

Take a drink, because it's more important to stay hydrated than almost anything else.

Once you've assessed the situation and decided what to do—probably stay put or hike out—then proceed step-by-step to do so.

If you're going to stay put, then set up camp to stay warm and dry. This is critical, and it's a whole lot easier to do that early on than to warm up or dry out after becoming cold or wet. Clothing is the key. Bring rainwear and extra layers of clothing in your pack.

Don't try to build a shelter. It will take several hours, and it's just about impossible to build a waterproof and windproof shelter out of natural materials. Instead, use the shelter you have brought with you. I recommend the 4-ml orange bag (see the equipment list), with a face-sized hole cut 8 inches down from one corner. I can put on all the clothes I've brought, get inside the bag, and stay fairly warm and dry. Plus, I'm visible because the bag is bright orange.

* These notes come from an article about Peter Kummerfeldt in the August 1999 *Field and Stream*. Kummerfeldt has been an Air Force survival teacher for 30 years.

Dangers: An Incomplete Primer

Grizzly **bears** do not currently live in the area covered by this book. They are, however, scheduled to be reintroduced into the nearby Selway-Bitterroot Wilderness. Should that happen, it might be wise to consult Stephen Herraro's book *Bear Attacks* on how to respond to an encounter with a grizzly bear. In general, assuming the fetal position with your face down and your hands behind your neck is considered an appropriate response to a grizzly attack.

Black bears live throughout the area. Because of hunting, most are so afraid of humans that when they sense one, they disappear. Black bear problems are most likely to occur around camps that are not kept clean and where food is left out, when the bears are hungry, or if the bear is surprised.

To prevent surprises, be proactive. Look for bear sign: claw marks on trees, scat, overturned logs. Let them know you are in the area by making noise that is easily identifiable as human when you hike. "Any noise that's not normally part of their environment," says Dan Davis of the CWNF. Bears also appear to notice movement, and bright ribbons tied to the top of a pack are noticeable.

Pepper spray is considered effective against bears. But it must be suitable for bears—not in the tiny containers sold as defense against people, and it must be sprayed from a short distance. It should be kept within easy reach; buried at the bottom of a pack does not help much.

Confrontations with black bears vary, according to Herraro. Most involve a question of food or space, in which case, simply backing away should end any attack by the bear. But black bears have been known to consider humans as food, and if an attack continues beyond a minor swipe or bite, that may be what's happening. In that case, fighting back would be a good idea.

Cougars also live throughout the area, and problems with cougars are increasing. Those problems tend to happen at the urban interface, says Davis. They generally involve young cougars and young children who are small enough to be considered prey.

When camping and hiking, keep a close watch on children. Should you encounter a cougar, don't run and don't turn your back on it. Pick up small children. Try to look as big as you can by stepping up on a rock or stump, or by spreading your coat over your shoulders to increase your silhouette. Be aggressive by throwing rocks or sticks and yelling at the animal. If the cougar attacks, try to remain standing and fight back. Kick, punch, go for the eyes. Pepper spray also works well to deter a cougar.

Moose are, arguably, the most dangerous animal out there. They normally don't consider humans a threat, especially when encountered on their terms. But an unexpected meeting can be dangerous. Davis met a cow moose one winter. She was down in a valley, while Davis was on snowshoes, far above. The moose took exception, which he knew when he saw her ears go back and the hair on her back stand up. (That's a bad sign on any animal, wild or tame.) "She was up the valley in a flash," he says. He spent some anxious moments with a tree between the moose and himself, until his companion distracted her.

Should you surprise a moose, move away. Don't threaten it by staring. Look to the side, don't make eye contact, and remain as nonthreatening as possible. And think about trees, for you can always use one as Davis did, or climb one if you're agile.

Rattlesnakes are found in the lower elevation areas and generally are most active from May to September. The Selway River is noted for them (hike 20).

A rattlesnake rattles as a warning when you're getting too close. Then it usually leaves the area, so you just need to wait until it's done so. If you don't wait long enough, as once happened to me, it will let you know by rattling again. It's a good idea to watch where you put your hands and feet, especially around rocks.

Treatment for rattlesnake bite is controversial. If you're on the trail, you're not likely to have antivenom. The current on-trail treatment consists of applying a loose, wide band—not a tourniquet, but about as tight as a watchband—between the bite and the heart. Keep the victim quiet. Keep in mind that many bites don't involve the injection of venom. Remember that you are about three times more likely to die from a bee sting than a snake bite.

Bees, wasps, hornets, and yellow jackets all sting. The most prevalent here are the bald-faced hornets that build the beautiful, gray paper nests in the trees, and the yellow jackets that live underground.

Benedryl will help all but the most severe reactions: two 25-milligram tablets for an adult, one for a child under 12. You can put something cold right on the bite to help reduce or slow the reaction, and you should remove the stinger, for it keeps injecting poison. A credit card or knife edge can be used to scrape the area to remove it.

If someone is going to have a severe reaction to a sting, you will probably see the signs within a few minutes: shortness of breath, redness, and swelling.

Ticks are most common from March until early June. Wood ticks are flat bodied, $3/8$ inch long, with eight legs that stick out to the sides. The adults and near-adults climb up grasses and low-growing plants in the spring, hold on with two legs, extend the other six, and hope a warm-blooded animal passes by to grab on to. Once they're successful, they'll climb higher looking for tender skin into which they gradually insert their mouth parts. You won't feel a thing.

To prevent ticks from attaching to you, wear clothes that fit snugly around the waist, wrist, and ankles. Wear light colors so you can better see them should they find you, and tuck your pant legs into your socks. Use an insect repellent containing at least 40% DEET around your ankles and lower pant legs. Even sun block is said to help deter them.

Inspect yourself each evening, for it takes several hours for a tick to attach. Especially check hairy places, behind the ears, nape of the neck, under a belt, strap, or elastic band. If you find one attached, pull it gently and steadily to remove. If the mouth parts remain embedded, remove them with a flamed needle or knife blade, then wash the area well and sterilize it if you can.

Some ticks carry Rocky Mountain Spotted Fever, which is caused by a parasite of the tick. Its symptoms appear three to twelve days later and include a severe headache, chills, muscular pain, fever, cough, and/or rash. Rocky Mountain Spotted Fever can be treated with antibiotics.

There is no documented evidence for Lyme disease in this area. It is carried by the much smaller deer tick.

Spiders found outdoors should cause no problems. All the nasty types that live in this area are found around human housing.

Poison ivy is the only one of the poison ivy–oak–sumac triumvirate that is found in the area covered by this book. It is a shrub here, 2 to 6 feet tall, with three shiny leaves near the end of stems. (It's actually a compound leaf with three oval leaflets, but it looks like three oval leaves.) The leaves may be beautifully colored in brilliant shades of red during the fall, and after the leaves fall, the white berries are good identifiers. In early spring, all you will see are white berries on slender, wooden stems. Poison ivy is found in moist areas, along streams and crevices, in the lower elevations of the region.

Should you touch poison ivy, rinse off the area as soon as you can. Soap helps, as does the tannin in tea, for the irritating substance is an oil. I've been told there's also a wash you can buy that will help.

Stinging nettle can give you a rash, and it really does sting, almost immediately. But there's relief. If you realize you've touched it, spit on the spot. Your saliva, or the enzymes in it, will help break down the formic acid that is causing the pain.

Stinging nettle stands 3 to 9 feet tall, usually in bunches, and especially in disrupted terrain. Its leaves are lance shaped and have coarse, saw-toothed edges. I think they look a bit like stretched-out mint leaves. The flowers are inconspicuous and hang in drooping bunches under the leaves. The formic acid comes from a gland, and the stinging hairs on the leaves are hollow and are attached to that gland. When you touch the plant, you break off the hair tip and release the acid.

Other Plants. Please note that there are poisonous plants in some of the areas covered by this book. Don't eat anything you can't absolutely and positively identify as edible.

Fire. If there are serious forest fires such as those we had in 2000, you won't be allowed to enter the forest. If you camp, especially on the Motorway, you are required by Idaho state law to carry a shovel and a pail of least one gallon size with you during the fire season—which includes anytime you would be up there.

Lightning usually takes the shortest or easiest pathway to the ground, so don't stand under tall trees or on ridgetops during storms. You also should avoid open areas, stands of trees in the open, and shallow indentations in cliffs. And put away your umbrella.

The safest place is at least 100 yards down from the crest of a hill, in a low spot or depression without tall rocks or trees nearby. Squat to make yourself even lower, making as little contact with ground as possible. Since lightning travels as far as 30 yards through the ground, stay a few yards out from the base of a cliff or the walls of a cave.

Sheltering in a heavy forest is relatively safe as long as you don't stand under the tallest tree or where it looks like there have been lots of strikes in the past.

If you're in a bad spot, set aside any metal. Although it won't attract lightning at any distance, if you were hit, the metal will cause burns.

Water. Don't drink it unless you treat it, for pure mountain streams aren't. The worst thing you probably would get from drinking the water is giardiasis. It is caused by *Giardia lamblia*, a small protozoan intestinal parasite that is not easy to kill. To adequately treat the water, boil it for 5 minutes, filter it through a 0.4 micron or smaller filter, or use iodine tablets. (The manufacturers of the tablets recommend a double dose to kill *Giardia*.) An interesting note: If a group of people drink water contaminated with *Giardia*, not all will show the symptoms and get sick. Those who do get sick, don't enjoy the experience.

Dehydration. Drink 3 to 5 quarts of water a day when outdoors. Without adequate water, your ability to efficiently function degrades rapidly. The symptoms include pale moist skin, dilated pupils, headache, nausea, and disorientation.

Hypothermia occurs when the body's internal temperature drops a few degrees below normal. It can happen quickly, as from a fall into icy cold water, or gradually over a long, wet hike. Most hypothermia occurs in mild weather, between 30–50 degrees Fahrenheit. Being wet, in the wind, tired, or hungry aggravate it.

The symptoms of hypothermia progress from uncontrolled shivering to disorientation and physical difficulties, such as fumbling hands or frequent stumbling, to drowsiness and apparent exhaustion.

Your body automatically starts to shiver to stay warm and restricts blood flow to the extremities so as to preserve normal temperature in the body core and vital organs, which means the hands and feet will get cold. These actions drain the body's energy reserves. If the causes of the cold are not alleviated, the cold can reach the brain; judgment and reasoning ability will deteriorate.

The basic treatment for hypothermia is to stop the cause of being cold and wet, if possible, and work to get the victim warm. Get him or her out of the wind and rain, and replace wet clothes with dry. Give warm drinks if he or she is mildly impaired, along with food and water. If seriously impaired, strip the victim down and put in a sleeping bag with another person or two, also stripped, to raise the body temperature again.

Shock is the result of blood loss or lowered blood pressure. The symptoms are paleness, cool skin, thirst, and a weak, rapid pulse. To treat, lay the victim down with his or her head slightly lower than the hips, unless there is a head injury, in which case the head should be higher than the hips. Raise the legs 10–15 inches and keep the victim warm.

Heat exhaustion happens when the body's cooling system has reached its limit. It starts with heat cramps, which are usually due to a loss of electrolytes, potassium in particular. Sports drinks replace these substances. If heat exhaustion progresses, the victim will be pale, clammy, and sweaty. Get the victim into the shade; cool by sitting in a creek or spraying with water. Don't give salt. Instead, give sports drinks. To help prevent heat exhaustion, wear a hat, drink plenty of water, eat properly, and avoid fatigue.

Think ahead when gathering together your equipment for hiking, both about first aid and about survival needs. The checklist I use each time I hike is reproduced at the end of this section.

Many magazine articles and hiking book chapters have been written about what you should take with you when you hike. Most offer a version of the ten essentials, and we're going to do the same, except our list is more extensive. As you check it against what you have, keep in mind the special nature of much of the hiking in this book: You probably won't meet anyone else out there, and if something goes wrong, you need to be prepared to help yourself. Even if you're planning to go only a couple of miles from the trailhead, be prepared to stay the night and to deal with basic first aid needs.

The Essentials. Carry these with you on all hikes.

1. Maps. The maps in this book are meant to be sufficient. But if you're planning ahead, reading this book while still at home or before you reach the Lolo, Montana to Lewiston, Idaho, segment of Highway 12, then buy the appropriate USGS and Forest Visitor Maps for the hikes you're planning. The USGS maps help you remain current as to where you are on the trail, and they help with the identification of the natural landforms you see. The Forest Visitor Maps help you identify what is in the distance.

2. Compass. If you stay on the short, well-used trails in this book, a map and compass aren't really necessary except as they enhance your enjoyment of the hike. But short, easy, well-used trails are good places to learn to use these tools or to hone skills for the future. So take them.

3. Knife. I gather the knife has multiple uses, though each person I've asked about their knife smiles a small smile and goes silent, as if those uses should be obvious, perhaps. Certainly a knife can be used to make small pieces of wood out of a larger piece, as kindling for a fire. It can cut a shirt into strips for tying a bandage or splint. It might be used for self-defense against an animal, whether four- or two-legged. Or, as one source suggested, it may only provide you with a bigger false sense of security than anything else you are apt to have with you.

4. Fire starter. There are a variety of these on the market that are small and lightweight. I always carry two, wrapped in plastic.

5. Matches. I carry two waterproof containers of the wooden, strike-anywhere variety.

6. Flashlight. Remember to bring extra batteries and bulb.

7. Extra water. Water purification tablets or a filter. Again, do not drink any water found in the area without treatment. (If the only alternative is serious dehydration, then the risk of drinking untreated water may be acceptable.)

8. Extra food. Food will boost your energy during a hike and help to prevent fatigue. I carry dry fruit, energy bars, and nuts as my extra food.

9. Extra clothing. I always carry a complete set of polypropylene long underwear (weight depends on the season), a warm hat, and a sweater-weight fleece jacket or sweater in my pack, all protected from the elements in waterproof bags.

10. A complete set of rainwear. Good quality keeps you drier from the inside out, in theory, if not in practice.

11. First aid kit with a manual (see below).

12. Whistle for signaling.

13. A waterproof bag that covers you. I have a 4-ml orange bag like those used for Adopt-a-Highway cleanups, with a face-sized hole cut 8 inches down from one corner. It's highly visible, and is something to enclose myself in should I need to stay out longer than planned, or should the weather turn wet.

14. Duct tape. What can I say? It can be used to fix an amazing variety of items. A few feet wrapped around a film canister is easy to carry, and plastic gloves can be carried inside the canister. (See First Aid Kit.)

15. A trowel for digging a hole in which to bury human waste.

16. Safety pins, chute cord, dental floss, needle. These are primarily for equipment repairs.

17. Especially if it's cold, a pad to sit on in case you have to spend time wrapped in the waterproof bag.

18. Sun protection and insect repellent.

19. Warm gloves. Nice if it's cold and you have to stay out longer than you had planned.

The First Aid Kit.

1. A small first aid manual, especially if you're not confident of your ability to perform basic first aid under pressure.

2. Ace bandage.

3. Sterile gauze pads, including a 5 x 9-inch Surgipad or other large, absorbent item.

4. Pain killers—aspirin, nonaspirin, and ibuprofen.

5. A few Benedryl tablets.

6. Moleskin for blisters.

7. Band-Aids.

8. Butterfly bandages or Steri-strips for holding lesions together.

9. Triple antibiotic cream.

10. Triangle bandage. Mine is made of Tyvek, which is both strong and lightweight.

11. Plastic gloves. You should not handle fluids from someone else without wearing gloves. A 35-mm film canister holds one pair.

12. Powdered sports drink.

13. First aid tape. (I don't carry this because I can use the triangle bandage, bandannas, or a ripped-up shirt to tie on a gauze pad.)

Packs.

Options range from tiny fanny packs to full-fledged backpacks. It's unlikely that all you should carry will fit into a fanny pack, and once loaded, I find them uncomfortable around my waist. However, it doesn't take a backpack to carry all this. A day pack of about 2,000 cubic inches should hold it all, with room to spare. One with a padded hip belt takes the weight off the shoulders and is more comfortable to wear.

Clothing.

I'm a confirmed wearer of natural fibers except when hiking or cross-country skiing. For those activities, I choose the synthetics, even for underwear. They dry from the inside and provide some warmth when wet. Wool also works, but is harder to find.

Think layers, then the clothing can be almost infinitely adjusted to the environment. My layers usually consist of a tank top, long-sleeved shirt, and sweater-weight fleece for the top. I also might wear a lightweight long-underwear top if it's cold. The bottom layer varies. I prefer either tights made of polypropylene and lycra combined with a pair of shorts or lightweight long pants, or heavier, long, convertible pants with bottoms that can be zipped off to produce shorts. If I need it, there's the long underwear set in my pack, and my rainwear provides the last, water- and wind-protective layer. I always wear a sun hat and carry a warm hat.

Boots and socks.

Hike with sturdy boots. They provide ankle support and foot protection on rough and uneven trails. Leather that you keep treated with waterproofing conditioners will provide as much protection from water as more expensive boots that have been treated with Gore-Tex.

I recommend wearing two pair of socks rather than one, a thin inner liner and a thicker outer layer. The inner socks wick the moisture to the outer pair and help to keep the feet drier. Although both pair of socks that I wear are wool, my feet really do stay dry and relatively cool, even on hot August days and even wearing my very substantial boots.

ALWAYS IN MARY'S DAY PACK
Emergency Bag

compass

knife

fire starter

matches—two containers, one with whistle

flashlight with extra batteries and bulb

orange plastic bag

duct tape on film canister with latex gloves in it

safety pins

water purification tablets

sports drink powder

First Aid Kit

manual

Ace bandage

gauze pads

painkillers

Benedryl

moleskin

Band-Aids

butterfly bandages or Steri-strips

antibiotic cream

triangle bandage

Other Gear

long underwear in a plastic bag

rainwear

fleece or wool sweater in a plastic bag

nuts

dry fruit

power bars

food for the day

map

water and extra water

bandanna

warm gloves in season

hiking stick

notebook and pencil

camera and film

sunblock

bug repellent

trowel

Ethics, Etiquette, and Responsibilities

The outdoors can take a lot of use but only if we treat it well. Although hiking is relatively easy on the land, in comparison to most other outdoor activities, it is not without consequence.

The most important thing is to always minimize your impact. Follow whichever wilderness mantra you prefer, even when you're not in the wilderness: "Leave no trace," or "Take only pictures, leave only footprints." This means taking no souvenirs and leaving all natural objects where they are. It means picking no flowers, taking no rocks, and minimizing your disturbance of life, whether flora or fauna.

Staying on the trail minimizes your impact. It keeps the disturbed area of the trail confined to a specific area, and cutting switchbacks leads to erosion.

And for goodness' sake, pack it in, pack it out. We're used to having our garbage taken care of for us. Outdoors, we need to deal with it ourselves. Please consider being proactive by carrying a small trash bag with you for picking up what others have left.

Dispose of human waste at least 200 feet from any water source. Dig a hole about 6 inches deep and bury it there, down where there are microbes that can degrade it. Toilet paper should be carried out with you. I suggest a double plastic bag kept separate from your food and water supplies.

If you meet horses while you're on the trail, make sure they see you and know what you are. Talking helps them to identify you. To let them pass, step off the trail on the downhill side, unless the riders ask you to do otherwise.

Check with the local Forest Service offices about hunting seasons. There are spring seasons and fall seasons. Except for the first week or so of elk season, I don't think they should cause a problem for hikers, but others feel that the spring turkey hunt might be of concern. Wear blaze orange to be sure you are seen.

Recognize that some areas are open to multiple use, and respect the rights of others to these legal uses.

Dogs can cause problems with wild animals, can even draw a bear to you. They also can chase wild animals, causing those animals to expend large amounts of energy that will have to be replaced. If you take a dog on the trail, keep it on a leash. Don't leave dogs locked up in a closed car while you hike; leave them at home.

If you go home with an increased appreciation for the trails you've hiked and want to help out, get in touch with your local Forest Service office. Most trails need more trail work than they receive. Volunteer trail work is done primarily by horsemen, bike, or off-road vehicle groups. I've been told, however, that getting together a group to help on a weekend may only make life difficult for the Forest Service professional who has to monitor you. He or she is not paid overtime and may not receive compensatory time for that day. Some Forest Service offices will let you volunteer on a work crew for a week or so, which is a good way to give back a little, help the hikers' reputation, become acquainted with some of the people in your local Forest Service office, and get to know a small area well. The National Forests also have a program called "Passport in Time" in which you can help by working with an archaeological crew.

Resources

United States Forest Service http://www.fs.fed.us.

For information on Lolo Motorway permits, specific hikes, visitor maps, hunting and fishing regulations, trailhead pass requirements, or other questions, see:

Clearwater National Forest, 12730-B Highway 12, Orofino, Idaho 83544, 208-476-4541 (main office and visitor information); http://www.fs.fed.us/r1/clearwater

- Powell Ranger District, CWNF, Lolo, Montana 59847, 208-942-3113.
- Lochsa Ranger District, CWNF, Rt. 1, Box 398, Kooskia, Idaho 83539, 208-926-4274.
- North Fork Ranger District, CWNF, 12730 Highway 12, Orofino, Idaho 83855, 208-476-4541.
- Rocky Mountain Research Station, 1221 S. Main, Moscow, Idaho 83843, 208-882-3557.

As of 2001, CWNF Visitor maps also are available at the Conoco Station in Kamiah; at Thom Cat and at Franks and Dales Cashway in Kooskia; and at the Riverside Sport Shop and Sunset Mart in Orofino.

Nez Perce National Forest, Route 2, Grangeville, Idaho 83530, 208-983-1950 (main office).

- Fenn Ranger Station, HCR1, Box 91, Kooskia, Idaho 83539, 208-926-4258.

Lolo National Forest, Building 24, Fort Missoula, Missoula, Montana 59804, 406-329-3750 (main office).

- Missoula Ranger District and Area Visitor Information Services, Building 24A, Fort Missoula, Missoula, Montana 59804, 406-329-3814.

USGS Maps. Dealers in any state can be found via http://mapping.usgs.gov/esic/map_dealers; or use http://www.usgs.gov; or call 1-888-275-8747 (1-888-ASK USGS). The following are some of the places that sell maps, either in person or by phone. If they cannot help, they may be able to suggest who can.

•Idaho Geological Survey, Controllers Office, Room 332, Morrill Hall, University of Idaho, Moscow, Idaho 83843, 208-885-7964.

•Army Navy Economy Store, Inc., 827 D. Street, Lewiston, Idaho 83501, 208-746-6430.

•Missoula Blueprint Co., 1613 S Ave. W, Missoula, Montana 59801, 406-549-0250.

•Oregon Dept. of Geology and Mineral Industries, 800 NE Oregon St., Box 5, Suite 177, Portland, Oregon 97232, 503-872-2750.

USGS maps for the CWNF are available at the Clearwater Forest's main office in Orofino, Idaho (see above).

Lewis and Clark Interpretive centers or visitor centers:

There is a large center in Great Falls, Montana—the Lewis and Clark National Historical Trail Interpretive Center, 406-727-8733. There should be several more centers by 2003, including at Lolo Pass; Hells Gate State Park in Lewiston, Idaho; in Clarkston, Washington; at Travelers Rest in Lolo, Montana; at Fort Peck, Montana; and at Pompey's Pillar, Montana.

Try the following websites for more information and links.

http://www.lewisandclarkidaho.org

http://lcbo.net

http://wshs.org

http://montanalewisandclark.org

Area museums with Lewis and Clark features:

Nez Perce National Historical Park in Spaulding, Idaho. It is located a couple of miles south off Highway 12 on Highway 95. 208-843-2261.

The Lewis County Historical Museum in Kamiah, Idaho, 208-935-2290, for the Chamber of Commerce. There is a mammoth at this museum.

Center for Arts and History in Lewiston, Idaho, 208-792-2243.

Nez Perce County Historical Society in Lewiston, Idaho, 208-743-2535.

Bibliography

Alt, David D. and Donald W. Hyndman. *Roadside Geology of Idaho*. Mountain Press Publishing Company, 1989.

Ambrose, Stephen E., *Undaunted Courage*. Simon and Schuster, 1996.

Boone, Lalia Phipps. *Idaho Place Names: A Geographical Dictionary*. Idaho Research Foundation, 1988.

Clearwater National Forest (CWNF) *Trail Guide*. Updated yearly.

Craighead, John J., Frank C. Craighead, Jr., and Ray J. Davic. *A Field Guide to Rocky Mountain Wildflowers*. Houghton Mifflin Company, 1963.

DeVoto, Bernard, ed. *The Journals of Lewis and Clark*. Houghton Mifflin, 1953.

Fazio, James, Mike Venso, and Steve Russell. *Across the Snowy Ranges: The Lewis and Clark Expedition in Idaho and Western Montana*. Woodland Press, 2001.

Hartig, Louis F. *Lochsa*. Kendall/Hunt Publishing Company, 1989.

Herraro, Stephen. *Bear Attacks*. Nick Lyons Books, 1985.

Larrison, Earl. J. *Mammals of the Northwest*. Seattle Audubon Society, 1976.

Moore, Bud. *The Lochsa Story*. Mountain Press Publishing Company, 1996.

Nussbaum, Ronald A., Edmund D. Brodie, Jr., and Robert M. Storm. *Amphibians and Reptiles of the Pacific Northwest*. University of Idaho Press, 1983.

Parish, Roberta, Ray Coupe, and Dennis Lloyd, eds. *Plants of Southern Interior British Columbia*. Lone Pine Publishing, 1996.

Patterson, Patricia A., Kenneth E. Neiman, and Jonalea R. Tonn. *Field Guide to Forest Plants of Northern Idaho*. General Technical Report INT-180. Ogden, Utah: U.S. Department of Agriculture, Forest Service, Intermountain Research Station, 1985.

Petrides, George A. and Olivia Petrides. *A Field Guide to Western Trees*. Houghton Mifflin Company, 1992.

Pojar, Jim and Andy MacKinnon, eds. *Plants of the Pacific Northwest Coast*. Lone Pine Publishing, 1994.

Ritter, Sharon Anelia. *Lewis and Clark's Mountain Wilds: A Site Guide to the Plants and Animals They Encountered in the Bitterroots*. University of Idaho Press, 2002.

Space, Ralph S. *The Clearwater Story: A History of the Clearwater National Forest*. Forest Service, USDA and the Clearwater Historical Society, Orofino, Idaho. U.S. Forest Service USDA, Northern Region-79-03, (234 pgs) Circa 1979.

Spellenberg, Richard. *The Audubon Society Field Guide to North American Wildflowers*. Alfred A. Knopf, 1979.

Wilfong, Cheryl. *Following the Nez Perce Trail: A Guide to the Nee-Me-Poo National Historic Trail with Eyewitness Accounts*. Oregon State University Press, 1990.

Author Biographies

Mary Aegerter is a freelance writer. She was born in Iowa, raised in a Chicago suburb, lived in the Boston area for twenty-five years, and moved west after a midlife graduate degree. After a couple of years of scientific research and a couple more years of teaching at a local college, she started hiking in earnest—and writing about it, too. She has been the hiking columnist for a local paper since 1995 and spent several years running the outings program of the local Sierra Club group.

Steve F. Russell is an Associate Professor in the Department of Electrical and Computer Engineering at Iowa State University. He was born in Lewiston, Idaho and spent his growing years at several locations along the Lewis and Clark Trail. He has lived at Lochsa Lodge, Weippe, and Orofino, all in Idaho, and in the Bitterroot Valley of Montana. Since 1986, he has been doing research on the historic trails of the Lolo Trail corridor: The Lewis and Clark Trail, the Bird-Truax Trail, and the Northern Nez Perce Trail.

He has appeared in "Echoes of a Bitter Crossing," produced by Idaho Public Television (1998), coauthored the companion IPTV website for "Echoes," and coauthored *Across the Snowy Ranges: The Lewis and Clark Expedition in Idaho and Western Montana*. Russell maintains a website on historic trails at www.historic-trails.com.